two roads

CHRIS CROWE

DESERET BOOK

Salt Lake City, Utah

Library of Congress Catalog Card Number: 94-70171

ISBN-10 0-88494-920-6
ISBN-13 978-0-88494-920-6

Printed in the United States of America
Publishers Printing, Salt Lake City, UT

10   9   8   7   6   5   4   3   2   1

Thanks to Anna, Cherie, Cindy, Debbie,
and Shauna, fine readers and critics all,
and to Elizabeth, who steered me to the
right road in the first place.

Two roads diverged in a wood, and I—
I took the one less traveled by,
And that has made all the difference.

—Robert Frost, *The Road Not Taken*

chapter 1

The rattling Honda Civic sped down the dark and narrow dirt road going fast.

Too fast.

The car's headlights cut a dim path through the night; its taillights glowed red in the cloud of dust that trailed behind it.

A sharp turn in the country road came up fast.

Too fast.

The driver had no time to brake or turn, so the car rocketed into the cotton field and rammed a concrete and steel irrigation gate. On impact, the driver smashed into the steering wheel, then whiplashed back into his seat. The crash jacked open the right back door, and the other boy clipped his shoulder on it as he flew out of the car and into the field.

The force of the collision catapulted the third passenger—the girl in the front seat—through the windshield and directly into the path of the car as it tumbled onto its side next to the irrigation gate.

Within seconds, the dust devil of shattered glass and dirt settled, and quiet darkness once again ruled the night.

Five minutes passed.

Ten.

Then the boy in the field stirred, and in the dim glow of one cockeyed headlight, saw the wreckage behind him. He blinked several times to clear his vision, then pushed himself to his feet. His shoulder throbbed, and he couldn't move his arm, but the growing worry about his friends brushed his pain aside. Stumbling to the car, he heard the moans of the boy inside and carefully dragged him from the wreck.

After laying the boy down, he staggered back to the car, and in the shadows saw the battered form of the other passenger, the girl with the flowing blonde hair. He dropped to the ground to embrace her, to clutch her in his arms hard enough to keep her spirit from slipping away, from leaving him.

But he knew, even as he held her, that she was gone.

That was when the adrenaline knocked the bottom out of his stomach. He trembled uncontrollably, choking for air, and through it all he prayed, wept, screamed for help but knew that it was too late.

Just as it had always been too late.

Jared snapped awake, wide-eyed and sweating and panting like he'd just run a marathon. He no longer counted how many times he had relived that nightmare—it had become a part of him, a part he wished he could forget.

The room was cold, as it had been every morning that week. He lay still a moment trying to get control of his breathing before he began the long and difficult fight to drag himself out of his *futon* and across the room to light the small kerosene heater that provided heat for the elders' apartment. In the quiet morning darkness he could hear the muffled movements of his new companion fighting jet lag and the urge to stay between the soft warm folds of the quilts a while longer.

If a light were on, he'd be able to see his breath in the frigid air of their apartment, and he knew from many mornings' experience that once he left the snug confines of his *futon,* the icy December air would bite through his wool pajamas and chill him before he even had a chance to get the heater started. He wanted to lie there just a moment longer to clear his head of the nightmare and to work up the guts to face another freezing morning. It was P-day and he had a greenbean companion to break in, so he couldn't linger any longer. With a shout, he threw back his heavy quilt, sidestepped the dark form of his companion still half-asleep on the floor, and raced to the heater.

The spark caught on the third attempt, and the yellow-blue flame in the center glowed while the heater filled the room with warmth and the acrid odor of kerosene. Jared hardly noticed the scent anymore, but his companion probably would find it unbearable for a few days at least. After waiting a moment to guarantee that the flame would keep burning, Jared wrapped his quilt around him, waddled to the rickety wooden table in the center of their dingy two-room apartment and grabbed his scriptures. Then to the front door to throw on the light switch. "*Ohaiyo gozaimasu!* Good morning and welcome to Japan, Elder. Time for scripture study."

Sitting as close to the heater as he dared, Jared opened his scriptures and pulled his quilt around him.

He was still in the Isaiah section of Second Nephi, and he couldn't help thinking that Nephi was rubbing it in when he gloated about glorying in the plain and simple words of Isaiah. For as much sense as it made to him, it might as well still be in Hebrew. But he had long ago decided that if he kept at it, running his eyes over the words often enough, it eventually might make sense to him too.

After a couple of verses, though, his mind wandered back to the nightmare. It had been the accident all over again: the breaking glass, the crunch and crash of metal, the spinning and confusion. He always saw it as an outsider, saw his own body thrown from the right side of the car, saw Rob smash into the steering wheel and snap back into the front seat, and saw Leisel, saw her launched through the windshield and land in the tumbling car's path.

Slow motion. Always terrifyingly, agonizingly slow.

He tried to scream, to reach out to stop it, to run to pull her out of the way before it was too late, but he was a helpless observer. Lately the nightmare occurred so often that he rarely needed his alarm clock to wake up.

Unable to read, he walked to the closet, dug out his stocking cap and pulled it over his ears. Then, with the quilt still tight around him, he slid open the door that led to the veranda of their third-floor apartment. The slap of the early morning winter stung him awake. He leaned against the railing and looked over the blue and grey tile rooftops of the houses below. It was still too dark to see the narrow roads between the buildings, but the soft glow of light seeping out from a few kitchen windows told him that others were up now too.

In the fuzzy darkness to the east, Jared picked out the silhouette of Himeji-jo, the centuries-old Japanese castle that dominated the city's landscape. In another hour, the streets would be alive with cars and buses and kids on bikes pedaling their way to school. But for now it was quiet and peaceful—and *freezing* cold—and Jared stood there pondering life, his mission, his friends back home.

His thoughts were interrupted by a knocking on the glass door to the veranda. The bleary face of his new companion, Elder Newcomb, peered through the frosty glass. Jared pulled the door open and stepped inside.

"Sorry," said the greenbean, "I didn't mean to interrupt your morning prayer or anything, but I just thought you should know that we're on the verge of asphyxiation here." He pointed to the heater. "It's incomplete combustion. That heater thingy's going to eat up all the oxygen in here and pump out enough CO fumes to suffocate us in an hour." He blinked several times, then squinted at Jared and said, "Maybe you better turn it off?"

"Turn it off and we can start storing our food in here instead of in the fridge. Don't worry about the gas, Elder, this place is drafty enough that we get a constant supply of fresh, clean, *cold* air. You'll get used to the stench of kerosene in a week or two."

Standing in the middle of the room, shivering in his new white cotton pajamas and bare feet, Elder Newcomb nodded without replying. His bottom lip quivered.

Jared waved his quad at his new companion. "Look, you can stand there in the pj's your mommy bought you and complain about the smell, or you can start acting like a missionary. Now it's shave and shower time, if you can handle the ice-cold shower. Study time's at 7:00 and breakfast at 7:30. I'm cooking."

The elder nodded, again without speaking, and turned to his suitcases to dig out his shaving cream and razor.

Jared watched him for a moment and shook his head. *Great,* he thought, *they've stuck me with a total wimp. That's all I need.*

Jared had breakfast cooking on their two-burner gas stove when his companion emerged from the bathroom, his hair damp and his face bright red. He walked over to the heater and sat down, shivering, in front of it.

And held his nose.

———

"This stuff is *mugi,*" Jared said as he slid a bowl of steaming boiled milled wheat in front of Elder Newcomb. "Throw some butter on it, hose it down with honey, and it's not too bad. You'll get used to it, just stay close to a toilet for the first few days. The stuff in the cup is *mugicha,* wheat tea. It's an acquired taste, but it's hot, and in this cold, you want all the hot you can get."

Jared folded his arms and nodded to his new companion. "Your turn for the prayer."

"In English?" asked Elder Newcomb.

5

"No, Swahili. Look, you're on your mission now. This is what they trained you in the MTC for, remember?"

The new elder mumbled a prayer in broken Japanese asking the honorable emperor to ordain the food they would humbly partake of so that it might bless their elbows and ears throughout the month.

Jared sighed an amen.

When the morning dishes were done, he showed Elder Newcomb how to wash clothes. "Only two shirts and one pair of pants will fit at the same time. Throw in a scoop of that powder over there, and turn the switch like this. When it's done, throw it all in the little bin next to the washtub and it'll spin it dry—and knot it all up at the same time. When that cycle's done, unravel your stuff and hang it out on the veranda to dry."

"But it'll freeze out there, won't it?"

"Not if you get it out while the sun's still shining this way. We can write letters while the wash is getting done, then eat lunch. After lunch we'll go grocery shopping."

Elder Newcomb started his laundry while Jared sat at the table, pulled out a pad of stationery, and started writing his weekly letters. He owed Brother and Sister Lee one, and he also planned to write to his bishop, his parents, and, if he had time, one to Rob Whitman. In the year and a half Jared had been in Japan, he'd never heard from Rob. Jared had written him often at first, then because he never received a reply, tapered off to a letter every month or so. He now wrote to Rob more out of habit than friendship.

By 10:00, Elder Newcomb joined Jared at the table. Like most new missionaries, this elder had a long list of people to write to, most of them high school friends and girls. "Got a few girls waiting for you, eh, Elder?" Jared couldn't help asking.

Elder Newcomb flushed. "Yeah, well, sort of. Only two or three are actually *waiting* in the sense that they're waiting for me to return in hopes that our relationship will continue. The others on this list are just friends, nice girls I don't want to lose contact with."

"Why?"

"You never know—the girls I think are waiting might not wait after all. And, you never know what two years will do to a girl, if you know what I mean. So I figure these girls are insurance. What about you?" He nodded at Jared's open day planner. "Have you got someone waiting?"

"Not really. As a matter fact, in the last few months, I've wondered if anyone at all will be at the airport to pick me up when I get back home."

"What, are you an orphan?"

"Not exactly. But my parents aren't members and they're not too thrilled about me wasting two years spreading Mormonism in Japan."

"Oh." Elder Newcomb was silent a moment. "Who are you writing to now?"

"My old girlfriend's parents."

Newcomb grinned and raised his eyebrows. "You must be on pretty good terms with them, but shouldn't you be writing her instead of her parents?"

Jared dropped his pen onto the notepad and leaned back in his chair to stretch. "Well, Brother Lee baptized me, so I guess we are on pretty good terms. He's one of the main reasons I came on a mission."

"So, you fell in love with his daughter, she talked to you about the Church, and you got baptized only to have her dump you, right?"

Jared didn't answer right away. He got up from the table, walked to the sliding glass door and stood there a moment looking out over the city. He hated breaking in new companions. "I did like her, liked her a lot, I guess, and yes, she definitely talked to me about the Church.

"As a matter of fact, there was a time when I couldn't get her to talk about anything else. But I got baptized after everything was all over."

"You mean after she broke up with you?"

CHRIS CROWE

He shook his head and turned around to come back to sit at the table. He looked Elder Newcomb in the eye and said flatly, "After she died."

Jared picked up his pen to resume his letter writing. He knew that before the week was over, he'd have to tell the whole story to his companion.

chapter 2

Elder Newcomb dabbed his chopsticks at the surface of the steaming bowl of noodles Jared had made for lunch. "What did you say this stuff was?"

"*Udon*. Noodles and broth."

"No raw fish or squid?"

Jared shook his head.

"You sure? See, my mother told me to make sure I watched my diet here in Japan. She calls me a sensitive eater 'cause when I eat fish it makes me itchy, but I've got this cream to use if it happens, but still, I have to be careful. Mom always checked my food to make sure it didn't contain any fish products, except for fish sticks—I always loved those, you know with tartar sauce and ketchup. But the thought of eating raw and slimy fish meat . . ." Newcomb shuddered. "Yuck."

Jared stared at his companion, wondering if he'd be able to put up with him for the next couple of months. "Do you always ramble like this?"

Newcomb shrugged and grinned. "Well, heh, heh, I don't know. I guess so. Mom always says I started talking when I was ten months old and haven't stopped since. But I've never thought of myself as overly loquacious, if you know what I mean. Just curious. Mom says I'm always asking questions and talking about new things—it's a sign of a healthy mind; inquisitive minds are the ones that learn the most. I remember when I was in third grade I had to do an oral report on a foreign country. And you know what? I chose Japan—talked a whole hour about it. I had pictures, maps, samples of Japanese candy. Mom helped me with it, of course, but the teacher said she'd never had a better-prepared oral report. So I guess I've been blessed, in a way, with the ability to express my ideas, and—"

"Be quiet and eat your noodles, Elder." Jared poked his chopsticks at Newcomb's bowl. "We need to go shopping after lunch."

By 1:00, the two elders were on their way to buy groceries.

As they neared the bus stop, Elder Newcomb asked, "So what happened to your girlfriend?"

Jared sighed. "I can't tell you about Leisel without first telling you about Rob."

"Her brother?" asked Elder Newcomb.

"Her old boyfriend."

They sat on a wooden bench beneath a bus stop sign. A few bikes and motor scooters whizzed by close enough to make the new elder pull in his feet. Jared ignored the traffic.

"Rob Whitman and I used to be best friends. I'm pretty sure he was the first LDS friend I ever had, although I wouldn't have guessed he was Mormon. He's one of those guys who's ashamed to be LDS, afraid kids will call him a goody-goody or something. Friends and fun are important to him—with fun being number one on his list. I think he always figured he could be wild in high school and then shape up in time for a mission."

"And did he?"

"No."

"So how'd you get to be friends with a guy like that?" asked

Newcomb. "My mom never would have let me hang around guys who might be a negative influence."

Jared shrugged. "My family moved across town that summer, and I had to change high schools. It was the first day of school, and we were in the same Senior English class."

* * * * *

The opening day of school at Mount Vista High School was hot, as it always was in Mesa in late August, and the new students, the sophomores, plodded around in flocks, clinging to their junior high school pals as they wandered the campus in search of their classes.

Jared Hills found his third period class, Senior English, and walked in. A few kids were already in the room; some whispered while others fidgeted at their desks. He chose an empty desk in the back of the room and sat down to wait for the bell to ring. A middle-aged woman stood in the front of the room writing her name, Ms. Hornbaker, on the chalkboard in perfect flowing cursive. When she finished, she turned around and rested her hands on the wooden lectern that stood in the front of the class, adjusted her glasses, and flashed a schoolteacher smile. The class quieted down, waiting.

When the bell rang, she cleared her throat and opened her mouth to speak but was interrupted when a student burst into the room.

"This Senior English?"

Ms. Hornbaker, her mouth still open, nodded.

"Great. I was afraid I'd never find this dumb class." He strolled to the front of the room and dropped his books onto the only empty desk, the one right in front of Ms. Hornbaker. "Sorry." He grinned and sat down.

Ms. Hornbaker asked the students to do the same thing they did in every class that day: introductions. First name, last name, hobbies. She went in alphabetical order, giving each student a turn.

Jared stood up when it was his turn. "I'm Jared Hills. Came here from Dobson High. My hobbies are sports."

"Which sports, Jared?" asked Ms. Hornbaker.

Before he answered, he sat down, anxious to have the class's attention off him. "Football and basketball."

"Football? What position?"

"Tailback, I guess."

Ms. Hornbaker smiled and called on the next student.

Jared doodled on his notebook while the other kids introduced themselves. Some he recognized from around town, but most were new to him.

One introduction remained, and Ms. Hornbaker nodded to the boy who had come in late. He was tall and when he moved, muscles rippled under his tight, blue T-shirt. His dark brown face and bleached hair obviously came from a salon, not from hard work in the Arizona sun. He stood up and faced the class, grinning and chewing gum at the same time. His head tilted a little to one side, bobbing slightly to an inaudible beat, and his eyelids drooped as if he were bored, but his eyes sparkled.

This guy loved the spotlight.

"I'm Whitman. Robert Whitman. Friends call me Rob. My hobbies, well, there's quite a few . . ." He paused to make sure he had everyone's attention. "But mainly they're parties, sports . . . and girls."

Most of the girls giggled. Ms. Hornbaker snickered too, then cleared her throat. "We don't need to hear about your love life, Robert, but which sports do you like?"

"I'm pretty good at all of them," he replied, "but my best sports are football and basketball. I'll be the starting tailback on this year's team."

"Oh, really? That should come as a surprise to, let's see . . ." She scanned her notes, then looked at Jared. "Jared Hills, didn't you say you were a tailback?"

He nodded.

"Well, Robert, it looks like you'll have some competition."

Jared glanced at Robert Whitman standing there, basking in the attention with his cocky, gum-chewing grin. Today was the first time he'd ever seen Whitman in street clothes. Before that, the only place he'd ever run into Whitman was on the football field or basketball court.

The bell rang, triggering a rush for the door. Jared was gathering his books when someone tapped his shoulder.

"Hey, don't I know you from somewhere?" It was Whitman.

"Probably," Jared said.

"Yeah. You played at Dobson. I guess you look smaller in real life." Laughing at his own joke, he looked over Jared's shoulder and winked. "Hang on, Leisel. I'm coming." He slapped Jared's arm and said, "Look, I'll see you at football practice after school. Stay cool."

He walked past Jared and put his arm around the girl who had been waiting near the door. She hooked her arm around him, and the two of them walked out of the classroom glowing like Ken and Barbie.

———————

For Jared, the worst part of football practice that afternoon was finding out Coach Lunt had assigned him the locker right next to Rob's. That meant that he'd have to put up with Rob's big mouth before, during, and after practice for the entire season. After their first practice, Rob blabbed for fifteen minutes about the great things he had done that afternoon. When it became obvious that Jared wasn't interested, he changed the subject.

"Yo, Jared, did you notice Leisel, that chick I was with after English? Not bad, huh? She's in my ward. That's one advantage of being a Mormon guy. We get the inside track with Mormon girls."

"Lucky you." Jared sat down and pulled on his shoes.

"So what ward are you in?"

"Huh?"

"What ward?"

"What's a ward?" he asked.

"Oh, come on. Don't tell me you're *that* inactive."

"What are you talking about?"

"Come off it. You know, a ward. Mormons. Latter-day Saints."

"Sorry, you got the wrong church, Whitman."

"No way," he said. "Jared's a Mormon name. You're a Mormon, man."

"That'll be big news to my parents. My dad hates Mormons."

Rob shook his head. "I can't believe it. You look totally Mormon, and I haven't heard you swear. Dang, I'll bet you don't drink or smoke either, right?"

"I didn't know Mormons had a monopoly on being good. But drinking? Yeah, I've had a few at home with my parents on holidays and stuff, but that's it. It's stupid for athletes, serious athletes, to drink. How about you?"

"Alcohol? Me? No way, man, I'm Mormon." Rob blushed, then grinned. "OK, maybe a couple drinks at a party now and then, but that's it. My dad would kill me if he ever found out."

"Mormons are into murder, huh?"

"No, stupid. It's a long story." Rob stood up and finished buttoning his shirt.

———

The next morning in English class, Jared noticed Leisel as she walked into class with two other girls, all three squeaky clean. *Momos,* he thought when he saw them. *You can spot Mormon girls a mile away.* Leisel was the tallest of the three, and the best-looking. Her blonde hair reached past her shoulders and framed a face that glowed when she smiled. *What she sees in Whitman,* Jared wondered as he admired her from his seat in the back of the room, *is beyond me. Maybe their church forces Mormon girls to hang around only with Mormon guys.*

Leisel noticed Jared looking at her and smiled. He smiled back and looked down at his desk. *What a waste,* he thought as class began, *for a girl like her to go with a jerk like Rob.*

Ms. Hornbaker had planned a get-acquainted writing activity for the day. "After I put you in pairs, I want you to interview each other, using five questions of your own, and then write a descriptive paper about your partner. Four hundred words, due tomorrow."

Jared moaned at the thought of a writing assignment so soon and at the same time wondered who he'd get paired with. Across the aisle to his right sat Sam Boggs, a kid who looked destined to spend most of his life on the street or in jail. Boggs slouched in his desk—his usual position—and glared up at Ms. Hornbaker through a strand of greasy red hair that hung over his eyebrows. When Boggs heard about the assignment, he muttered an obscenity—his usual vocabulary—and glared at Jared.

"This rots, man. What a stupid class."

Ms. Hornbaker was already calling out the pair assignments, and Jared had missed hearing his partner's name. He looked around, hoping he wouldn't get stuck with Boggs or Rob Whitman.

"Hey, you're Jared, right?" Leisel slid a desk next to his. "I think we're partners."

"Uh-oh, Jared," sneered Boggs as he got up to find his partner. "Looks like you got a Momo on your hands. Better watch out or she'll try to convert you."

"Knock it off, Boggs."

"What's with you? You like *Mormons?*"

"No, I just don't like jerks."

Boggs didn't faze Leisel. "Why, Brother Boggs," she said in a phony Southern voice, "I'm just doing a little old-fashioned proselytizin' here to save this poor sinner's soul. Just be patient, honey, and soon as I have time, I'll send the missionaries over to your house too."

Boggs scowled and stomped off to the other side of the room.

"Creep," Jared said as he adjusted his desk to face Leisel.

"Maybe he had a warped childhood," she smiled.

"More like a warped adolescence."

"Think I could save him?"

"Fat chance. He'd probably machine-gun any Mormons who came near his house. What is it about you guys that bugs him so much?"

"Is this one of your interview questions? 'Cause if it is, you only have four left."

"I get it. You want us to get down to work, right?"

"Well, we do have an assignment to get done, and it is due tomorrow."

"All right. I guess I'll go first. What's your name?"

"Leisel Marie Lee."

"Age?"

"These are killer questions, Jared. Give me a minute to think about this one." She rolled her eyes. "Let's see . . . seventeen and a half."

Jared made a note on his paper. "Where were you born?"

"I don't mean to criticize, but you're not going to have much to write about if you keep asking me dumb questions like that. Don't you know anything about interviews?"

"I suppose you do?"

"Well, I do know that if you want to find out about someone, you have to ask them questions that will give them a chance to talk about themselves. Like this: What is your greatest goal in life?"

Jared thought for a minute. "You mean this life, right now, or life after high school?"

"*Life*. All of it."

"I haven't thought about it much. I want to have a good job, lots of money to take care of my family and to pay for a nice house, a good car. But I don't want a career that eats up my whole life. I want to have time to spend with my kids and to do some of the things I want to do."

Leisel scribbled in her notes as Jared talked. When he stopped, she asked, "Question two: What kinds of things do you like to do?"

"Geez, this is like a real interview."

"It *is* a real interview. Answer the question, please."

"I like to listen to music, play sports—mainly football and basketball. In the fall when the weather cools off, I like to hike and camp up in the Superstition Mountains. Used to do that a lot when I was a kid."

"You still are a kid. Question three: What do you want to be when you grow up and why?"

"That's two questions, and I don't know the answer to either one. I guess I want to do something good, you know, help people."

"OK. Question five." Leisel stared into her notebook and said quickly, "What do you know about the Mormon Church and would you like to know more?"

"Two questions again. That's cheating. But just to show you I'm not a jerk like Boggs, I'll answer them both. Nothing and no thanks."

She sighed and looked up from her notes. "Well, that's about it for me."

Jared glanced at the clock and saw that only a few minutes remained in the class. "Look, you still owe me two and a half questions. How about if I ask you them at lunch?"

Leisel's face lit up. "Great. I'll meet you outside the cafeteria."

After the bell rang, Rob met Leisel at the door. Jared hung back at his desk to avoid complicating things, but Leisel managed to complicate things all by herself.

"Hey, Jared," she called from the doorway, "don't forget our lunch date." She waved and walked into the hallway, her running shoes squeaking on the tile while Rob stopped for a moment to glare at Jared before he left.

If looks were nuclear, thought Jared, *I'd be radioactive waste.*

chapter 3

"You know," Elder Newcomb pushed back his glasses with his index finger, "I knew somebody like Rob once. Well, not exactly *like* your friend, but he played chess and he was a classmate of mine. I always wanted to play football, but my mom wouldn't let me. She thought the guys who played were too rough. But I always figured I had some athletic ability, and I wanted a chance to prove myself. So in high school, I went out for the chess team. Only I had to quit that because it gave me headaches."

Jared tried to hide his growing frustration with his new companion. *It's just the first day,* he told himself, *I can adjust. Charity. I've got to learn to love this geek. Somehow.* He looked at Newcomb rambling on about high school. *This is going to be really hard,* he thought.

"Anyway," Newcomb continued, "when I was on the chess team, one of my teammates was named Ralph, and your friend Rob sounds kind of like him. Not that they acted the same way or anything, but I also met Ralph in English class and his first name and Rob's both start with R."

Jared was grateful when the bus hissed to a stop in front of them because it stalled Newcomb's boring monologue. Elder Newcomb plopped into the nearest seat and Jared slid next to him. Newcomb sat with his face pressed against the window commenting on things the bus passed.

Got to learn to love this guy, thought Jared, *because if I don't, I'm going to go absolutely bananas.*

After a few minutes, Newcomb turned back to face Jared. His nose was red and dripping with moisture he had rubbed off the window. "So," he said as he mopped his face with his handkerchief, "what happened at lunch with you and that girl?"

Jared was relieved to have a chance to do some talking. "When I finished eating, I went looking for Leisel. We finished my interview and then talked for a while, and the more I looked at her, the more I thought, wow, this girl is gorgeous. I wanted to ask her out, but I didn't know if Mormons could date heathens like me.

"Anyway, there was going to be a dance that Friday, so I asked if she was planning on going. She said yeah, so I told her I was too and then she smiled." Jared paused a moment and drew a deep breath. "Man, I loved her smile. I think that's when I really got hooked on her.

"Rob showed up while we were still talking. Leisel ignored him for a few minutes and I could tell that he was getting pretty steamed. Finally he stepped in front of her and said, 'How long you going to spend talking to this bozo?' Then she got really mad—red face and everything—and told him he didn't own her. Rob said he didn't want to own her, he just wanted to trust her. Well, they went back and forth for the rest of the lunch period. When I went to my next class, they were still there yelling.

"I didn't see her again until the next day in English class."

* * * * *

Class hadn't started yet, and Jared was putting the finishing touches on his interview report when Leisel showed up.

"Sorry about what happened at lunch yesterday."

"No problem."

"No, it *is* a problem. Rob's a real jerk sometimes."

"Sometimes? I thought it was 24/7."

She sat down in the desk behind him. "Well, he has his moments, but he can be really sweet when he wants to be."

"That's hard to believe. He sure wasn't very sweet at football practice yesterday. Look at this." Jared pulled up his shirtsleeve to reveal a large greenish-blue bruise.

She gasped. "Rob did that?"

"Got me when I wasn't looking. Two or three other guys took even worse shots than I did. Rob went wild in tackling drill, and Coach loved it of course. If you two have many more fights, I'm afraid Rob'll put our whole team in the hospital." Jared nodded to the doorway. "Here comes old sweetie pie now."

Rob limped into the room. He had a small bandage over his left eye and his cheekbone was swollen and purple.

Jared grinned at Leisel. "He's not the only guy who knows how to knock people down."

For class that morning, Ms. Hornbaker surprised everyone by making them read their descriptive papers aloud. Most were witty caricatures of classmates, a few were boring, some were serious descriptions, the kind of thing Ms. Hornbaker had wanted them to write.

Leisel's was one of the serious ones. She first described Jared's appearance: about 6'1", sandy-brown hair, athletic build. Then she got corny and started using all the information from yesterday's interview— that he wanted to have a good job and raise a family and wanted a career that allowed him to help others. That drew a few hoots from his classmates—"Family man, family man," called out one kid—but not nearly as many as Leisel's conclusion.

"In summary," she read, "Jared Hills is a fine young man, one I would certainly like to get to know better."

Jared slumped in his chair as the class laughed and razzed him. "Whoa-o, Jar-ed, you are hot!"

Sam Boggs reached across the aisle and slapped him on the back. "Hey, Jared-boy, sounds to me like there's a little Mormon romance in your future."

Jared ignored him and muttered to Leisel, "Thanks a lot. Geez, Leisel, you made me sound like a Cub Scout."

When the catcalls and snickers stopped and Ms. Hornbaker got the class calmed down, the readings continued. Leisel's paper had surprised Jared. What she had said in her essay—did she really think that about him? Did she like him, or was she just being funny?

When Ms. Hornbaker called on Jared, he sat up straight and began to read. He had titled his paper "The Mormon Madonna," and described Leisel as "the siren of Mount Vista High School, a voluptuous beauty who will undoubtedly leave a trail of broken hearts behind her when she graduates." The paper ended with, "She wants to get married, of course, to a nice Mormon man, have seven kids, and spend the rest of her life at home changing diapers and dreaming up new ways to serve whole wheat." His paper had gotten a few chuckles, even one from Ms. Hornbaker, but the whole time he read, he felt Rob's stare burning into him.

It wasn't the only thing he felt in his back. From her seat behind him, Leisel had been drilling the eraser end of her pencil into his spine while he read. "Not nice, Jared," she hissed into his ear when he finished. "Mormon Madonna?"

"Hey, I was just kidding around," Jared whispered over his shoulder, afraid to face her.

She didn't answer.

When the bell rang, she left without saying anything to Jared. Unfortunately, Rob did.

"You're really a jerk, Hills." He stood too close to Jared, challenging him. "Where do you get off saying stuff like that about Leisel?"

Jared backed away. "Hey, it was just a joke. She knows I was kidding."

"Oh, yeah? Well, I didn't see her laughing. She's one of those people who doesn't like to be teased about her religion. So just leave her alone, OK?" Rob turned and left without waiting for an answer.

———————————

Jared's house looked like most of the other houses in his subdivision in East Mesa: a run-down split-level with one palm tree, one orange tree, and a double garage filled with bikes and lawn equipment and boxes and golf clubs, everything but cars. As he walked up the driveway, he saw his mom's car, but not his dad's. He heaved a sigh of relief and pushed open the front door.

The musty smell of stale cigarette smoke irritated his nose. His dad smoked a lot; Jared could hardly recall ever seeing his father without a cigarette hanging from his lips, but his mom had quit a few years ago. Even though she wouldn't admit it, Jared knew she had quit more for Jared's sake than for her own.

"Hey, Mom, I'm home." He trotted up the stairs to his room, tossed his backpack on his bed, and headed for the kitchen where he knew he would find his mom fixing dinner.

"How was practice, hon?" She smiled without looking up from her cooking.

"All right, I guess. It's a lot more work than last year was."

"Got much homework tonight?"

"A little. What time's Dad going to be home?"

His mother went to the cupboard, took out two plates and carried them to the table. "Late." She didn't look Jared in the eye when she answered. She never did when she wanted to hide something from him.

"Is he gone again?"

She bit her lip and nodded quickly.

Jared swore under his breath. "Do you know where? For how long?"

She sat down in her chair and let out a long shaky sob. Then she inhaled to control her quivering voice. "Oh, I'm sure he won't be gone long. He . . . he left a note." She nodded toward her bedroom. "Said it'd just be a couple days this time." She managed a smile, but it just made her look older and more tired.

"Dang it, Mom! How can you stand it?"

Without answering, she stood up and went back to the stove. "Dinner's just about ready. I hope you're hungry because there's lots of spaghetti here." That signaled the end of their conversation about Dad.

So many times before, it seemed like all of his life, Jared's mother had refused to hear or say anything negative about her husband and his "publishing business." His father owned a small print shop, and several years ago had started taking in night work for radical groups who hired him to publish their hate flyers and propaganda. A few years ago, they started paying him extra to distribute their materials and eventually he even started going to their rallies and meetings.

Jared never really understood why or when his dad had changed, but he first noticed it when he entered junior high. The night before his first day of seventh grade, his dad came into his room and tossed a stack of pamphlets on his desk. "Read these, son. You're going to meet all kinds of people in junior high school, and some of them are dangerous. Lots of them are. And I don't want you associating with them." He looked at Jared hard. "You're a good kid, and I don't want your mind—or your life—getting polluted by any undesirables."

After his father left the room, Jared leafed through the papers on his desk. He recognized them as his father's shop's work, but the titles shocked him: "Are Blacks Human?"; "Are Mormons Christian?"; "Do You Know What Your Children Are *Really* Learning in School?"; "Will the Jews Inherit the Earth?" Every single pamphlet attacked a minority group. The tone of the words and the accusations they presented made Jared feel sick. After skimming a few, he gathered them all up and threw them in his wastebasket.

He didn't talk to his father about it for a long time. His dad wasn't the kind of father you could talk to about many things, and Jared knew from sore experience that it wasn't healthy to disagree with him. But near the end of ninth grade, he felt he had to say something. What his father was doing was wrong—even if it wasn't illegal—and it embarrassed and shamed Jared.

His dad had just returned home from distributing a batch of hate publications at a shopping center parking lot on the other side of town. Whenever he came back from his distribution runs, he was excited and agitated.

It was dinner time, so after he washed his hands at the kitchen sink and lit a fresh cigarette, he joined Jared and his mother at the kitchen table. "Had a little trouble tonight." He reached across Jared for the salad bowl. "Some punk kids tried to stop us. Kids about your age, son." He set the bowl down and started eating. "We just about had all the cars covered when Jack saw some kids on the other side of the parking lot tearing up our flyers. He yelled at them, and when I saw what was happening, so did I."

He took a long drag on his cigarette and set it on the ashtray he kept by his plate. Jared and his mother ate silently. They knew better than to interrupt Dad when he was excited.

"A couple of them ran off right away, but this one kid didn't. He just kept pulling our flyers off windshields, tearing them in half, and stuffing them into a bag. I worked on getting my row covered while Jack went over to straighten the kid out.

"Well, in a few seconds, I could hear them yelling pretty loud." His dad laughed. "Stupid punk wouldn't back down. So Jack pushed him around a little, you know, just to scare him off." He held out his empty glass to his wife. "Get me a drink, will you? Anyway, the little jerk took a swing at Jack. Well, then I figured I better get over there and help out."

Jared looked up from his plate. His face flushed, but he managed to control his voice. "What did you do?"

His father looked surprised, then chuckled. "We just roughed him up a little. Nothing serious. And he can't do a thing about it 'cause *he* threw the first punch."

Jared glowered but remained silent.

"That bother you, son?"

"He was just a kid."

"Kids gotta learn to mind their own business."

"Yeah, but, Dad, that stuff you print and put around—" his father's hard look scared him—". . . I mean, you've got to admit, it's pretty obnoxious."

Jared's mother gasped and looked from Jared to her husband to her plate.

His father ground out his cigarette in his salad and said slowly, "Look, son, let's get one thing straight. Our society is sick enough without it being overrun by losers and weirdos. I'm doing my part to make things better." He leaned forward and stared hard at Jared. "And I sure don't need my son to tell me what to do or what to think. If you're going to turn into some kind of slobbering loser lover, you and me are going to tangle.

"I don't want to hear another word about this from you—ever. And I definitely don't want you mixing with people who are polluting our society."

"Yeah, but, Dad, some of those people might be my friends at school. I don't see anything wrong with—"

His father's slap knocked him out of his chair.

Jared's dad stood now, confused and angry. "Can't I get any respect in my own house?" He glared at his wife, then at Jared. "I don't want to hear that kind of garbage from you ever again, understand? And you better never, *ever* let me find out you've been making friends with those kinds of people." He kicked his chair away from the table.

"I'm going out for a drink," he said to his wife. "And I hope you can talk some sense into your son before I get home, 'cause if you can't, I'll have to knock some into him."

Jared never talked to his father about it again. And in recent months, he rarely saw his father because his meetings and distribution runs took up more and more of his time. Occasionally, he would be gone for days, traveling to Southern California, New Mexico, or Utah to attend rallies or spread hate publications.

Jared hated what his dad was doing but always felt relieved when he was gone. He hated even more what it was doing to his mom. He knew that the tension between father and son tore her up, and that her husband's long absences and growing fanaticism worried her.

But even though Jared despised his father's business and the way he acted, he wanted to love him—he was, after all, his father—but his father's activities had separated them so much that, even though he knew he should, he felt no love for the man.

After helping his mom do the dishes, Jared went upstairs, turned on his radio—something he could do only when his dad was gone—and started on his algebra homework. Five minutes later, he tossed his pencil down and sighed. He couldn't concentrate tonight. All the stuff happening at school bothered him. Rob was ready to punch him out. He liked Leisel Lee, a Mormon, but knew if his dad ever found out, there'd be *real* fireworks.

Jared flopped onto his bed, closed his eyes and tried to think pleasant thoughts. Leisel and her smile. Leisel and her essay about him. He wondered what she had really meant in her essay. If she liked him . . . well, that would make life pretty sweet, even life with a crazy dad.

Then he remembered *his* stupid essay and Leisel's reaction. "I hope I haven't already blown it with her," he muttered out loud.

chapter 4

"Oh, man, your dad's one of those anti-Mormons?" Elder Newcomb whistled. "How's he feel about you being on a mission?"

"He writes once a month." Jared leaned forward and rested his arms on the seat in front of him. "Well, 'writes' isn't the right word—but he sends me stuff every month. Anti-Mormon pamphlets, anti-Japanese garbage, that kind of junk. Never a note or anything personal, though. Never a single word."

"Uh, Elder Hills?" His companion shifted in his seat. "Have you been keeping those things, you know, the stuff your father sends, in our apartment?"

"I just toss it in the box next to the bookshelf. Why? You want to read some?"

Elder Newcomb shook his head so hard his glasses almost came off. "But do you think it's a good idea to have those kinds of things in our apartment? I mean, what would the mission president say?"

"What can he say? I'm just keeping my dad's letters. Besides, I never read the stuff and never plan to."

"Then why keep it?"

Jared took a deep breath and let it out slowly. "I don't know. Maybe it's because I don't want to throw away the only evidence I've got that my dad still cares, or at least *thinks,* about me. And I keep hoping—maybe it's all just a fantasy—but I hope that my dad will change somehow. Or if he doesn't, that I'll be able to learn to love him even though I hate what he does. He's sure not making it easy." Jared rested his forehead on his arms.

"I think I know what you mean. When I was in ninth grade, there was this guy, a dumb football player who sat next to me in math and was also in my PE class. He always tried to cheat off me during math tests, and when I wouldn't let him he'd threaten to pound me at PE. I spent most of my ninth grade PE classes trying to keep away from him. But I always tried to be nice to him, even though he was a real jerk."

Newcomb wrinkled his nose and said, "Have you ever noticed how so many football players are jerks? My mom used to say it was just their egos and that in reality they were envious of guys like me who were intellectually talented. She said most of them relied on their brute strength to hide their other faults and that's why they liked to pick on me. Anyway, I've always tried to be charitable towards them, but sometimes I just wonder if guys who play football are capable of understanding charity . . ."

Jared looked up at his companion. "I played football, Elder."

Elder Newcomb paled. "Oh, yeah, that's right. Well, uh, maybe it was just football players at my school. I certainly didn't intend to make careless stereotypes. My mom always told me to make sure not to judge people too quickly, and sometimes—"

"Elder?"

"Yeah?" Newcomb looked anxiously at Jared.

"Turn it off for a while, will you?"

Elder Newcomb nodded, and as the bus wound through the narrow streets of Himeji, the two rode in silence.

They got off the bus at Miyuki-Dori, a narrow shop-lined street in the heart of the city.

It was nearly 3:00 when they finally emerged from the shopping
street, each with a plastic sack full of groceries. They stopped at a tiny
shop to have a cup of hot chocolate to warm them up before going home.

"Hey, did you ever go to that dance?" Elder Newcomb squinted
through his glasses that had steamed up when they entered the little
restaurant.

"Huh?"

"You know, with that girl, Lisa, or whatever her name was."

"Leisel. Yeah, well, it took me a while, but eventually I went to one."

"Was she there?"

"Yeah." Jared stared at the chocolate granules in the bottom of his
cup.

"Was that guy there? That jerk who liked her?"

"Rob?" Jared nodded and smiled a little. "They came together."

*   *   *   *   *

Jared wasn't able to go to the dance he had originally planned on
because his father had grounded him. Two weeks passed until Jared's
father was out of town again, and that meant he'd finally be able to go to
a dance without any hassles. "Go and have a good time," his mother had
said that evening. "It's good to make friends at your new school." His dad's
response would have been different, more like a half-hour tirade on the
evils of dances, rock music, and high school punks.

For a few days after Jared had read his essay in class, Leisel had completely ignored him. In the days that followed, though, she gradually
warmed up but still hadn't spoken to him much. He had been extra nice
to her, no Mormon jokes, no teasing, but he could still sense a barrier
between them.

This morning she had said hello to him when she sat down, and good-bye when class was over, and that was enough to renew his hopes. Jared had made up his mind to apologize to her at the dance and say whatever he had to say to convince her he was sorry. He desperately wanted another chance to be friends with her and hoped she'd be there.

At the dance Jared sat along one wall of the darkened gym with some friends from the football team. That night's game—an easy victory—and girls were their main topics of conversation.

"Oh man, there's Michelle Taysom. Hold me back, guys, I think I'm in love!" Vince Shumway, their offensive tackle—and the biggest kid in the junior class—threw his arms into the boys sitting on each side of him. "I swear, guys, I'm going to ask her to dance tonight. I mean it."

Tanner Farnsworth laughed and pushed his arm away. "Get real, Vince. She's not going to dance with a whale." He dodged Vince's elbow. "And besides, she's a *senior*. Probably doesn't even know you exist."

"No probably about it," said Jared. "She's so far out of your league you'll need a satellite hookup just to talk to her."

Vince dropped his arms into his lap and sulked. "I know it, guys, but what can you do about true love? And I'm big for my age; maybe she'll think I'm a senior."

"Seniors don't have peach fuzz." Tanner tugged on a wisp of hair on Vince's chin. "And seniors can drive. Even if she does dance with you— no, let's really stretch it: even if she falls in love with you, what're you going to do after the dance, walk her home?"

"I can see them now," said Jared. "Vince and Michelle Taysom walking into the moonlight with Vince's mountain bike between them. Pretty romantic, Vince. I think you ought to go for it."

"Come on, guys. Even juniors can have a little romance, can't they?"

"Yeah, but Vince," said Tanner, "you gotta be realistic. You can't start at the top when you're at the bottom. Look, there's Brooke Stapley. She's a sophomore. Go ask *her* to dance." Tanner grinned at Jared. Brooke's beauty made *seniors* melt at her feet, and she was one of the most popular girls in the sophomore class.

"Yeah, go on, Vince," said Jared. "What have you got to lose?" He tried not to laugh. "She might even like big guys."

Vince sat up. "You guys really think so? I mean, I don't want her to shut me down in front of the whole school . . . but she is cute."

"Cute?" Tanner punched him on the arm. "She's a total babe, Vince. Go for it before I do!"

Tanner and Jared pulled Vince to his feet and sent him lumbering toward Brooke and her circle of friends.

"Man, you're too cruel," said Jared as he watched Vince standing outside Brooke's circle of admirers, waving his hand in the air to get her attention. "This might set him back years, Tanner."

"He's too huge to get hurt by a little rejection. And he might as well get used to it. Fat dudes just don't have a chance with sweet babes like Brooke."

"What kind of guys do?"

Tanner grinned. "Me, of course." He pointed to where Vince stood pawing the floor with his right foot while talking to Brooke. "Here it comes, here it comes. She's going to roast him."

But Brooke smiled warmly and nodded to Vince. They couldn't hear what she said and watched in amazement as she took his hand, led him onto the dance floor and danced with him. Tanner slapped his hand over his eyes. "Man, I can't believe this. It's got to be a joke."

When the song ended, Brooke and Vince stayed on the floor, chatting quietly, waiting for another song.

"This is unreal," said Jared. "She's going to dance with him again."

After three dances, Vince walked back to his buddies grinning and glowing like he had just been named all-state. "Hey, guys, thanks a million." He flopped down on the chair between them, closed his eyes and sighed. "I'm in love, dudes. I mean, I'm totally in love. She's awesome."

Tanner could hardly stand it. "What did you say to her? Geez, Vince, I've known her since junior high and she never once would dance with me. Don't tell me she likes fat guys?"

Jared slapped Vince's thigh. "Come on, Romeo, what's your secret? How did you do it?"

"Natural charm, guys. Face it, a body the size of mine just oozes charm."

"More like sweat." Tanner poked Vince in the stomach. "Cut the bull and tell us how you did it."

"Well, she used to be in my ward when my dad was bishop. She remembered me from Primary and stuff."

"Mormon connection," said Jared. "I knew there had to be something."

"I should have known." Tanner looked over the dance floor. "She was probably just doing her monthly service project. See, Jared, there are some advantages to being Mormon." They were still teasing Vince when Tanner waved across the floor at someone. Jared turned and saw Rob waving back.

In the weeks since school had started, Jared and Rob had arrived at a grudging mutual respect. Both were talented athletes and realized that, if for no other reason, they should at least get along for the sake of the team. In some ways, Jared envied Rob's talent and confidence, but he still found it difficult to put up with Rob's cockiness, even if it was, as Rob liked to say, "No brag, just fact."

"Are we going to have to put up with him?" said Jared. Then he saw Leisel behind Rob as they walked over to him and his friends. "Leisel's with him?"

"You know Leisel Lee?" Tanner asked.

"She sits behind me in English class."

"You're lucky. Rob keeps a pretty tight rein on her. They're both in my ward, and it's a miracle if I even get a chance to talk to her without him around." He looked at Leisel and sighed. "Can't say I blame him, though."

Rob's appearance at the dance complicated things for Jared. He wanted to talk to Leisel alone and had to figure out how to get Rob out of the way for a while. Vince was the answer.

"Hey, Vince, I need to talk to Leisel for about ten minutes. Can you keep Rob out of here that long?"

"Easier said than done. You know how he is around her."

"Well, tell him about your recent romantic conquest. Tell him you won't block for him anymore." He handed Vince a five-dollar bill. "Tell him whatever you want—just keep him tied up for ten minutes."

"Five bucks." Vince clutched the bill and grinned. "Yeah, great idea. No sweat, Jared."

Rob walked up and slapped hands with his three teammates. "Hey, what's happening?"

Vince grabbed Rob's shoulder. "Oh, man, you won't believe what just happened." He pulled Rob to the other end of the gym to tell him the details of his adventure with Brooke Stapley. Rob resisted for a moment, but once Vince wrapped his huge arm around Rob's shoulders, there was no escape.

"What's with Vince?" Leisel asked as she sat down between Jared and Tanner.

"He's excited," said Jared.

"And love struck," said Tanner. He told her about Vince's success with Brooke.

"See, Jared," said Leisel when Tanner had finished, "it pays to come to dances. You never know who you'll make friends with." She smiled at him. "Anyway, I'm glad you finally made it to one. I was starting to think you had some sort of phobia or something."

"No phobia, just a crazy dad."

"Well, I'm glad you're here. I've been wanting to talk to you."

"Watch out, Jared." Tanner elbowed him in the side. "You don't want Rob seeing you talking to his girlfriend."

"I'm not his girlfriend," Leisel snapped. "And I can talk to whoever I want to."

"OK, OK. Sheesh, don't have a cow." He raised his eyebrows at Jared, and Jared frowned, signaling to him to leave them alone. Tanner got the message. "I can tell when I'm not wanted."

"It's not that we don't want you around, Tanner," said Leisel, "it's just that Crystal Craig is over there, and I think she wants to talk to you."

"Crystal? Really?" Tanner looked across the gym and saw her wave and smile at him. "Hey, thanks, Leisel. See you guys later."

"Are you still mad at me?" Jared asked as soon as Tanner had left.

"It depends. Did you mean any of that stuff in your essay about me?" Leisel wasn't smiling now.

"Well, I meant all the good stuff." Still no smile. "But the stuff about your religion, hey, I didn't mean to hurt your feelings or anything. I'm really sorry."

Finally, she smiled. "That's good to hear. But remember something, Jared Hills. My church is important to me, really important, and I don't like to be teased about it, OK?

"And I don't get mad, I get even." She punched him on the arm as hard as she could.

"Ow! OK, OK. No more Mormon jokes. Quit the abuse already."

Jared saw Vince dragging Rob out the gym doors into the hallway and decided to press his advantage. "Hey, Leisel, do you dance with guys you slug?"

She smiled and stood up. "Only if they ask me."

"Uh, you wanna dance?"

"How can I resist such an eloquent invitation?" She took his arm and led him to the dance floor.

It was his lucky night. The music changed to something slow, giving them a chance to talk as they danced.

"I just wanted to tell you," said Jared, "I liked your essay—even if it was a little corny."

"I didn't think it was corny. I always write what I think without wondering whether it's corny or stupid. If it's the truth, I don't worry about it. It was true, wasn't it?"

"Yeah, I guess so. I just didn't expect you to put it all in your essay and then read it out loud." Jared cleared his throat. "But I wanted to ask you something else—what you said at the end, was that true?"

"I didn't memorize that essay, Jared. What did I say at the end?"

He was glad that gym was dark. She wouldn't see him blush. "You know, that part about wanting to get to know me better."

Leisel smiled and looked down. "Yes," she said. "It was. It is."

When the music stopped, they walked back to their chairs. "Rob says you're a pretty good fullback, one of the best he's ever played with," said Leisel.

"That's easy for him to say now that he's got the tailback position, *my* old position, sewed up. What else does old Rob say?"

She plucked at a loose strand of blonde hair as she talked. "Oh, lots of things. He talks about you a lot lately."

"Plotting murder?"

"Murder? He likes you. As a matter of fact, I think you're the first guy I've ever heard him say nice things about. He's pretty competitive, you know."

"Pretty? The guy's a maniac. I've never seen anybody take sports so seriously."

"I wish he'd take other things as seriously." Leisel looked sad.

"Oh." Jared's heart sank. "So you'd like Rob to take you more seriously?"

"Me?" She laughed. "Are you kidding? That's the one thing besides sports he already takes too seriously. No, I wish he'd start to realize how important church is."

"Doesn't he go?"

"He's there every Sunday, he has to be—his dad is our bishop." She looked out at the dance floor. "But it's his attitude. It's like he doesn't even care about it at all."

"If he's going every Sunday, what does it matter?"

"There's more to our church than just attending meetings. I don't know. It's kind of complicated. But I worry about Rob sometimes."

"Why don't you just go to his dad and tell him that Rob's a jerk? Let him straighten Rob out."

"That's one of the problems. Bishop Whitman is a great guy, but Rob can't see that. Mormons joke that the worst kids in wards are always the bishops' kids. Well, Rob's doing his best to make that true and it's driving his dad crazy. Bishop Whitman and I both know that deep down inside, Rob is a good guy and all that, but if he walks the edge too long, he might fall off."

"What's that mean?"

"He'll lose his testimony. Become inactive. Cause his parents and himself a lot of misery."

Jared saw Rob and Vince approaching. "Here comes Mr. Misery now." When he saw how sad Leisel looked, he added, "Look, if there's anything I can do, you know, to help Rob stay off the edge, well, let me know. He's really not such a bad guy."

Leisel perked up. "Just be his friend, will you, Jared? He always puts down most of his Mormon friends as nerds and goody-goodies. But he likes you, and I think you're a good influence on him."

Be Rob Whitman's friend? He'd rather stick his head in a beehive.

But for Leisel . . .

"I'll do it." Jared figured he could get along with anybody who wasn't a bigot or a wimp. Rob, despite his nuclear ego, certainly wasn't a wimp and, as far as Jared knew, wasn't a bigot either. And who knows, maybe on the way to becoming Rob's friend, he might also become more than a friend to Leisel. That's what he wanted, right then, more than anything.

chapter 5

Jared and Elder Newcomb had finished their P-day dinner of curry rice and were getting ready to go out and do some missionary work. Dressed in his white shirt and tie, Jared sat at the kitchen table thumbing through his appointment book, waiting for his companion. He looked at his watch. Elder Newcomb had been in the bathroom for more than twenty minutes, and Jared was growing impatient.

"Come on, Elder, it's time for you to get introduced to real missionary life." He got up and pounded on the bathroom door. "We've got an appointment for 6:30 and if you don't move it, we'll be late."

Elder Newcomb emerged from the bathroom with a face white as milk. "Maybe you'd better go without me. I'm not feeling so hot." He plodded to the kitchen table and sank into one of the chairs.

Jared resisted the urge to grab Newcomb by the shoulders and shake his molars loose. Their appointment with the Terauchi family was one he had worked on setting up for months. To cancel it would be unthinkable.

"Don't be stupid," Jared said. "I can't go without you. We're *companions*, remember? Two by two?" He glared at his companion. He knew he should have charity for the greenbean, but knowing it and having it were two different things. "Look, Bishop Nagano referred this family to us. Do you realize how often we have a chance to teach an entire family? Do you have any idea how badly this ward needs some new blood, a new family? You can't be sick. You just got here!"

Newcomb sat with his elbows on the table, running his quivering hands through his hair. "Can't we go tomorrow night?"

"No, we can't go tomorrow night. Get a grip, man, this is Japan. Taricha works six days a week, twelve to fourteen hours a day. We can't just . . ." Jared stopped. His hands shook and he knew he was on the edge of his temper. Losing it wouldn't help either one of them. He took a deep breath and continued. "OK, dude, what's the problem? Was it the curry? I've got some antacid."

Newcomb shook his head.

"Headache?"

"No."

"Fever?"

Again, the elder shook his head.

"Then what is it?"

"I don't know," he whimpered. "This isn't what I expected. It's freezing cold and the people are so different and I can't understand a thing anybody's saying and I'm sure they won't be able to understand me." He slumped forward on the table. "I can't do it," he sobbed. "I should have never come here. I should have never come."

Great, Jared thought. *A crybaby, a mama's boy.* He fought the urge to scream at his new companion, jerk him out of his chair, and pound him into submission. But his anger passed. Jared knew from experience that he couldn't change someone by getting mad. It sure hadn't worked with Rob. It probably wouldn't work with Newcomb either.

*   *   *   *   *

By the end of the football season, the tension between Rob and Jared had diminished to the point that most people considered them friends.

Not good friends, not yet, but more than nodding acquaintances. With Leisel's encouragement, Jared became more tolerant and Rob had become kinder. But even Leisel's determination that the two become friends didn't do as much to cement their friendship as did an incident in their final game of the football season.

Mount Vista's archrival was McKinley High. The two schools were perennial contenders for the state football championship, and their coaches were bitter enemies who many suspected received more satisfaction from beating each other than from winning championships.

The intensity of the practices leading up to the McKinley game surprised Jared. Coach Lunt had impressed on them that even if they had won all their other games—which they hadn't—a victory over McKinley was what made a season truly successful.

"This is our state championship," he told them before the game. "We don't have a shot at the play-offs, but this is the game you'll remember all year. Win it, and you can savor it for twelve months. Lose it, and it will haunt you all year long."

After the first quarter, it was clear they'd have no trouble winning the game. With the huge holes opened by Jared and the offensive line, Rob ran with abandon, racking up several long runs and two touchdowns in the first ten minutes. From his fullback position, Jared added a score and the quarter finally ended with Mount Vista leading 21–0.

As the second quarter began, Rob and Jared stood on the sidelines watching their defense dismantle McKinley. "Who-ee! This is *fun*." Rob slapped Jared on the back. "When I get back in there, I'm going to rub it in their faces. Let's make this a game to remember."

For the next two quarters, Rob continued to run free, eluding the increasingly frustrated McKinley defenders and finding the end zone almost at will. After every play, Rob taunted his opponents. When he scored, he danced in the end zone and pointed the ball at the players he had beaten. Each time he was tackled, he bounced up from the pile and tried to shake the hand of the player who had managed to tackle him. "Hey, good job, buddy. You got me that time. Must be your lucky day."

By the end of the fourth quarter, the lopsided score and Rob's taunting had infuriated the McKinley players. "Better back off, Rob," Jared warned in the huddle. "These guys are getting sick of you."

"Is that why they're slapping my hand away instead of shaking it? I thought maybe I just smell bad."

"You do," said Jared. "But you're also being a jerk. Just carry the ball and keep quiet or these guys will kill you."

"They'll have to tackle me first," Rob said before the huddle broke.

The play was a right sweep. Rob took a pitch from the quarterback and sprinted through an opening in the defense. He accelerated down the sideline, sidestepping one defender and running past two more. Finally a McKinley player closed in, trapping Rob between the sideline and the defenders behind him. But instead of simply forcing Rob out of bounds, the McKinley players joined in a gang tackle that slammed him into McKinley's team bench.

The referee threw a flag for the vicious late hit, but the McKinley players didn't care. For several seconds, Rob remained motionless. Then he turned his head from side to side, untangled his legs from the bench, and wobbled to his feet.

"What's the matter, Whitman, getting too rough for you?"

Rob swore, threw the ball to the ground, and limped toward the field.

"Hey, hot dog, you don't look so great now." A McKinley player shoved Rob onto the field. Even dizzy and hurt, that was more than he could take. He spun on the player with arms swinging.

And triggered a brawl.

Jared was one of the first Mount Vista players to Rob's rescue. He ran into the swarm of players, shoving bodies out of the way and dodging fists, hoping to find Rob and drag him to safety.

Two McKinley players held Rob near the bench while a third

punched him in the stomach. Rob's eyes were glazed and his body hung limp in their grip. Jared dove into them, knocking Rob free and sending the McKinley players into the bench. He scrambled to his feet, grabbed Rob by his jersey and dragged him through the mob toward the sideline.

By then the referees and coaches from both teams had begun breaking up the fights. As Rob stumbled back to the Mount Vista sideline in Jared's grasp, he looked at Jared and mumbled, "Thanks, man," before passing out completely. Jared and a teammate dragged him the rest of the way to the bench where the trainer looked him over.

"Couple of loose teeth, bruises. He got his bell rung, but he'll live. Probably have a headache and some pain when he wakes up. Which ought to be any second now." The trainer snapped an ammonia capsule under Rob's nose and waved it back and forth.

"Huh?" Rob jerked awake. "Get that away from me," he moaned. He blinked and wiped the blood from his mouth. "Oh, man, I feel like I got shredded."

"You almost did, stupid," said Jared. "Those guys were trying to kill you."

Rob swore. "If they hadn't hit me from behind, I would have stomped 'em all. Cheap shots."

"You threw the punch."

"Only after they nailed me out of bounds. What a bunch of losers." He dragged the back of his hand across his mouth again and looked at the blood smeared there. "Somebody ripped on my head, and all I remember is seeing you dive into us and then drag me onto the field."

"Couldn't stand to see a wimp like you getting pounded by a bunch of McKinley dudes, so I dragged you out."

"Didn't have to, you know."

"Yeah, I know." He sat down beside Rob and slapped him on the thigh pad.

"Well, thanks, man. Really." Rob didn't say anything more, but they both felt the barrier between them dissolving.

———————

Rob and Jared lingered in the locker room after the game, long after the other players were gone. They had a late start getting cleaned up because after his end-of-the-season team speech where he screamed about the bench-clearing brawl and then praised them for beating McKinley, Coach Lunt called them both into his office and spent twenty minutes chewing them out about sportsmanship, football, and manhood in general.

"You two have tons of potential," he said when his anger finally passed, "and I don't want you to waste it fighting people. Play hard. Ignore the trash mouths on other teams. Let your actions on the field talk for you, not your fists or your mouths." He stared at them. "Now get the heck out of here," he said, snapping a towel at them as they left the office.

After they showered and dressed, Jared and Rob sat on the bench in front of their lockers, too tired to make the effort to go home, and both disappointed, though they wouldn't admit it, that the season was over. They talked for a while about games and plays and next year's team before Jared looked at his watch and realized he was late.

"Hey, man," he said, "I got to get out of here. My dad will kill me if I'm home late."

"Relax," said Rob, "I know how to deal with dads."

"Not my dad."

"Look, we just played our last game. I'll give you a ride home, and on the way we can stop off at a party to celebrate kicking McKinley's bootie."

"I don't know. I told my mom I'd be home as soon as I could."

"So call her. She was a kid once. Look, I promise I'll have you home by 12:30, 1:00 at the latest. Ask her."

Jared reluctantly agreed. Using the phone in the coaches' office, he

CHRIS CROWE

called home. His dad was still at work, so his mom gave him permission to go. "Have fun, son," she said. "But be careful and don't stay out too late."

"Promise, Mom. Thanks." He met Rob in the parking lot. "She said OK."

"Let's roll, then," said Rob as he started his car. "It's party time!"

Rob's weather-beaten Honda Civic spun out of the parking lot before Jared even had a chance to close his door. They were a block down the street before he finally got the door closed and his seat belt on. "Man, you're crazy. Where'd you learn to drive?" asked Jared.

Rob jerked the steering wheel and wove between two lanes. "What makes you think I ever learned?" When he saw the look on Jared's face, he laughed. "Hey, don't sweat it. I haven't had any wrecks—yet." He screeched to a stop at a stop sign.

"You're nuts!" Jared shouted over the noise of the car and the radio.

"Not nuts. Kamikaze. I drive a Japanese car. I have no fear of death. Banzai!" He sped down the local streets and out onto Stapley Road.

Jared was relieved no cops stopped them.

The party was in high gear when they arrived. As they approached the house, they could hear the thump-thump of the heavy bass music and see the front windows of the house pulsate with the sound. Party sounds— music, laughter, people talking—spilled out the open door and into the night.

This was Rob's element and he soon disappeared into the crowd, slapping hands, shouting greetings to friends, and laughing at others' jokes. Jared stayed near the front door for a while, trying to find some people he knew. Finally he headed for the kitchen where he found Vince Shumway.

"Hey, Jared, my man, have some food. They've got tons." He pointed to trays and bowls of food that filled the counters.

"I should have known I'd find you here." Jared grabbed a handful of chips and pulled up a chair next to Vince. "How's the party?"

"Boring, man. Brooke couldn't come."

44

"Any other guys from the team here?"

"Lots of them. Mostly they're downstairs on the Xbox. Some are out back on the patio, but it's kind of wild out there. Drinking and that kind of junk. I stay away from those guys."

Jared looked around. "You seen Leisel?"

"Are you kidding?" Vince nearly choked on a mouthful of tortilla chips. "She doesn't come to these parties. I don't either, usually. Matter of fact, I'm about ready to split. Need a ride?"

"No, I came with Rob."

"Better plan on staying a while. That guy's a real party animal."

Jared grabbed a can of soda and wandered through the house checking out the party. It seemed to him that most of the people were having fun, even if he wasn't. He didn't like the uncomfortable feeling he had: guilt, boredom, loneliness, he couldn't put his finger on it. He eventually joined some of his teammates at Xbox for a while, then got bored and around 12:15 set off in search of Rob.

He found him on the patio sitting at a round table with several other guys building a pyramid of empty beer cans. As they worked, Rob kept up a running monologue about the McKinley game, including exaggerated details of his big plays and the big fight.

"See, five McKinley guys were holding me while another dude was trying to take shots at my stomach." Rob paused and reached for a can of beer and took a swallow before continuing. "And I just did a kung fu kick that sent him flying." Everyone laughed, and Rob noticed Jared standing there, listening.

"Hey, Jared. My hero! Come here and tell these guys how you played Batman today and saved my hide. This man was a total stud. He came flying in—bam!—and sent the bad guys into the dirt. Come on, Jared, have a seat."

Jared sat down next to Rob, and Rob pushed a can of beer in his direction. "Have one, bud. Celebrate."

"No thanks." Jared felt his face redden.

"Come on, how do you expect to celebrate without a little drink?" Rob frowned, then slapped the table. "Oh, yeah, I forgot. You don't drink."

"What? Are you Mormon, Hills?" asked Russ Baker, another varsity player.

"Hey," said Rob, "*I'm* Mormon."

"Yeah," said Russ, "but you don't count. Why don't you drink, Hills?"

"It's got nothing to do with my religion. Just don't like it, I guess."

"Give me a break," Rob said. "One beer won't hurt you."

Russ scowled at Rob. "The guy doesn't want to drink, alright?"

"Yeah." Jared held up his soda can. "This is fine, really."

"It's cool." Russ turned to Rob. "Back off, man. No sense corrupting him too."

The conversation picked up again, and the party wore on. Jared dropped several hints to Rob that he needed to go home, and Rob kept telling him they'd go in just a minute.

When they finally got into Rob's car, it was nearly 2:00 and Jared was fuming. "You're a jerk, man. You knew I had to be home by 12:30."

"Relax. It's cool."

"It's not cool. You're not cool."

Rob put his key in the ignition but didn't start the car. "Let's not get personal. You didn't have to come to this party, you know."

"You didn't have to keep me waiting." Jared's voice grew louder.

"Relax. I'll get you home OK."

"I can't believe you." Jared snatched the keys out of the ignition. "You barely got me here in one piece. You think I'm going to let you drive me or yourself home when you're full of booze?"

"Not booze, just a few beers."

"It's all the same, stupid. What's your problem?"

Rob's face turned red. "What's *your* problem? I have a few beers and a little fun, and you flip out. You're not my dad, man, so back off. Now give me the keys so we can get out of here. I don't want you to get in trouble with your mommy."

"I'm not letting you drive."

"Give me the keys, Jared."

"No way."

"Stop being such a jerk! Give me the flippin' keys!"

Rob lunged for the keys and Jared threw them out his window. He grabbed Rob's arm and held it.

"You're acting like a total idiot, all I want to do is—"

Rob kept trying to shake his arm free.

"Will you listen to me!" Jared turned Rob loose. "You're half drunk. I'll get the keys and I'll drive you home." He released Rob's arm and swung his door open. "Maybe my mom can pick me up at your place."

As he walked to pick up the keys, Jared's mind spun. Rob was from a good family. His dad—at least according to Leisel—was a good man, not a jerk like Jared's. They had plenty of money. Rob was smart and talented. He had everything Jared would like to have, but he didn't care about any of it.

The ride to Rob's house started out as a shouting match. Jared did his best to yell some sense into Rob, and Rob did his best to out-shout Jared. Rob just wouldn't listen, and after five minutes, Jared had quit yelling. They rode the rest of the way to the Whitman's house in silence.

Jared parked Rob's car in the Whitman's driveway, yanked the keys out of the ignition, and tossed them in Rob's lap. "Let me use your phone to call my mom, OK? Then I'll get out of here."

He followed Rob as he staggered into the Whitman's dark house. Rob led him into the kitchen where he switched on a light, pointed to a phone, and slumped in a chair. Jared made the call and was on his way outside to wait when Rob spoke.

"You know, you really tick me off sometimes."

Jared paused in the doorway without answering.

"But I like you, dude. You're good for me, and I think," he paused to rub his forehead, "I think you saved my neck twice today. Thanks, man."

Jared left Rob's house feeling better than he had expected to. The night was crisp and dark and quiet, and he was glad for the quiet because he wanted to sort out his feelings. He couldn't figure out Rob Whitman. Why was he so anxious to reject the good things around him? Why did he, as Leisel had said, so willingly walk the edge? *It's funny*, Jared thought, *that a guy who knows better goes out of his way looking for trouble.*

Seeing a flash of headlights down the street, Jared stepped to the curb to meet his mom, but gasped when he saw his dad's car stop in front of the Whitman's house. The interior of the car was dark except for the ominous glow of his dad's cigarette.

He wanted to turn and run, but he knew that would be stupid. What would he tell his dad, how would he explain why he was so late? The blare of the car's horn brought him back to his awful reality.

"Get in the car!" his father yelled.

Jared got in.

His father slammed the car into drive and screeched into the street. "Do you know what time it is? And I don't care what your mother said, you know *I* don't like you going to parties with scum from your school. You been drinking?"

Jared shook his head.

"Speak when I ask you a question!"

"No."

His father swore. "Parties."

"It was just some guys from the team. We beat McKinley tonight and they wanted to celebrate the end of the season. We're seniors, Dad."

"Seniors. But you're on a team with a bunch of mongrels. Who knows what kind of stuff you've picked up from them. We should have put you in a private school, one where you wouldn't have had to mix with minorities and cult kids. Then I wouldn't have to put up with this garbage.

"What kind of party was it?"

"I already told you: guys from the team, some kids from school."

"And *you* figured it was OK to stay out all hours, huh? Didn't you tell your mother you'd be home by 12:30?"

"Yeah, but this friend of mine, the guy I went with, he didn't want to leave, and by the time I got him out of the party, he was too drunk to drive, so I had to drive him home."

"Sounds like you'd better be more careful about who you call your friend. Now listen to me, Jared, and listen good 'cause I'm only going to say this once." His father's face grew serious as he peered through the windshield. "This kind of stuff happens again and it's the *last* time it happens, understand?" His hands twisted on the steering wheel. "'Cause if I can't make my own son mind then I don't need a son anymore. You got it?"

"Yes, sir," Jared nodded. The only sound in the car the rest of the way home was the country music playing on the car radio.

chapter 6

Jared did what he thought he should do, not what he wanted to do. What he wanted to do was drag his companion out of his chair, down the steps of their apartment building, and bounce him all the way to the chapel for their appointment with the Terauchis. What he did was step out onto the veranda and into the icy night air to look over the city's lights. He gripped the railing, took a deep breath, and bowed his head, whispering a prayer asking for inspiration on how to help his new companion.

He also asked for special strength to keep him from pounding the snot out of Newcomb.

When Jared went back inside, his companion was kneeling at the kitchen table. His shoulders still trembled, but Newcomb was obviously deep in prayer, so Jared left him alone.

Newcomb finished in a few minutes and pulled himself back into his chair. He pushed his glasses back in place, then took out his handkerchief, wiped his forehead and blew his nose loudly. "Elder Hills," he said, "I've got to apologize." He wiped his nose again with the back of his hand before he continued. "I think I can handle it tonight. Well, I hope I can.

Maybe if we take it slow I'll be OK. Will I have to do any talking in Japanese tonight?"

"Tell you what, Elder, I'll take care of all the discussions and you can say the prayers. Can you handle that?"

Newcomb fumbled at his scripture case and pulled out a worn 3x5 card. "OK if I use my MTC prayer notes?"

"Just don't let the Terauchis see them. Prayers are supposed to be spontaneous."

Newcomb drew a shaky breath and sighed. "OK then, I think I can handle it." He stood up from the table. "Yes, I can do this. Let's go. I'm ready to start missionary work."

"Great, but one thing before we go—"

"Oh, right. We need to have a prayer."

"No, you need to zip up your zipper. Then prayer."

The two missionaries made it to the chapel on time and waited in the foyer for the Terauchi family to arrive. "This isn't so bad. I can do this," Newcomb repeated as they paced the entryway to keep warm.

Jared stepped outside and looked up and down the street in front of the chapel. No Terauchis in sight. There was no answer when he called them on the pink pay phone that sat in the corner of the foyer.

By 8:30 he knew they'd been stood up. He slammed his fist into his hand. Even though broken appointments were common, it still made Jared mad when people, good people who would blossom in the gospel, did everything they could to avoid embracing it.

"Looks like they're not coming, huh?" Elder Newcomb grinned with relief. "Guess we might as well head back to the apartment and start getting ready for tomorrow. Maybe we can have some hot chocolate or something. Tell you what," he patted Jared on the back, "I'll share some of the Oreos I brought from the MTC."

Jared nodded, pulled his coat tight around him, and went outside with Elder Newcomb, now buoyant and cheerful, following behind him.

Back inside their apartment, they sat at their kitchen table drinking the watery hot chocolate Newcomb had made. Elder Newcomb was still bubbling with relief over the cancelled appointment. "You know," he said, "this isn't so bad, missionary work, I mean. I can do it. Sure, my Japanese is still kind of weak, but I'll get better. I can do it." He grinned at Jared who sulked across from him. "Hey, don't be so down, man. We'll find some new people to teach tomorrow."

"It's not that easy," Jared said. "There's half a million people in Himeji and we get about sixty at sacrament meeting every week. With my last companion we tracted for three weeks before we even had a chance to—"

"Hold it, Elder. The Lord will help us, and besides," he smiled, "I just got here, remember? Let's not talk about negative things, let's talk about something positive."

"Like what?"

"Girls."

"I've been a missionary too long—I don't know anything about girls anymore."

"Tell me about your old girlfriend—Alissa?"

"Leisel."

"Yeah. Tell me how you guys finally got to be together, and I want to hear how she got you interested in the Church."

"Well," Jared sighed, "things started warming up between me and Leisel after Rob got drunk at a football party. She always hated that kind of stuff."

*   *   *   *   *

Leisel and Rob had a tremendous fight when she heard about his getting drunk. At church the Sunday after the party, Rob had tried to explain everything to her, but she avoided him until he finally cornered her in the back of the church near the baptismal font. An argument started and escalated until Leisel finally ended it by shoving Rob through the curtain and into the empty font.

Rob smoldered for days after that, refusing to talk to Leisel and speaking to Jared only when he had to at basketball practice.

And that's when Jared really started to get to know Leisel. It started with evening phone calls about Rob and what she should do about him. Then they started hanging around each other at school. They even went out for burgers after a couple basketball games—not exactly dates because Leisel's younger sister, Michelle, had tagged along.

A few weeks after their big fight, Jared sometimes saw Leisel talking to Rob at school, and usually Rob seemed to be listening, not arguing.

"I kind of feel sorry for Rob," she told Jared one night. "He's really mixed-up right now. He thinks it's OK to party and have fun while he's in high school and then repent right before he goes on a mission. And he always thought our relationship was more than it really was. I've been trying to explain to him that I don't hate him, and that I still care about him as a friend. To me, he's a lot like a brother. I've known him a long time and love him, just not romantically."

"How's he taking it?"

"Pretty good, I guess. Rob's never had any trouble getting girlfriends, so he's not going to die of loneliness." She paused. "I told him we've been going out."

"Great. Now he's going to want to kill me."

She shook her head. "Even though he's hurting now, you're still one of his best friends. I told him that I'd like us all to stay friends. And I think his dad talked to him too, you know, about how life goes on and all that."

As Christmas vacation approached, Leisel became the closest thing to a girlfriend Jared had ever had. Rob seemed to have gotten over his breakup with Leisel, and daily basketball practices helped things return to normal for Jared and Rob.

"Can't have a grudge for too long against the guy who passes me the ball so I can score zillions of points," said Rob one day after practice. "Just do me a favor, Jared."

"Yeah?"

"Stay away from my next girlfriend, OK?"

———

Lunch at Mount Vista High was more than just a chance to wolf down a few hundred calories and kick back for forty-five minutes before returning to the classroom grind. It inspired students to come up with new and creative ways to describe indigestion. It also gave them time to hang out with their friends and catch up with the latest school gossip, to realign, on a daily basis, the pedigree charts that kept straight who was dating whom, and to crank out last-minute homework assignments.

During lunch Rob and Jared hung out with the jocks that occupied the patch of lawn immediately in front of the cafeteria. The early December air was crisp, cool enough to give the people who had lettered in fall sports an excuse to show off their new letter jackets.

Not far from the jocks—sometimes their circles intersected—stood the Mormons, a melting pot of band kids, jocks, and cowboys. The druggies, when they were on campus, occupied a shady spot near the library at the far corner of the courtyard. Sam Boggs often hung on the fringe of their group, flitting from one gap to another like a hummingbird hungry for nectar.

Today, though, the druggies were paying attention to Boggs. He stood almost in the center of their loose circle, pointing at the jocks and Mormons, waving a pamphlet as he spoke. The kids around him laughed periodically, a couple even whistled and shouted something that Rob and Jared heard but couldn't understand.

"Stupid druggies," said Rob. "I don't know why they even come to school."

"Maybe they're looking for trouble," said Vince Shumway. "Let's go over there and rattle their chains a little."

"Might be fun," said Rob, "but why risk getting in trouble here at school?"

"Forget them," Tanner said. "We got to get this New Year's Eve party planned before lunch is over so we can spread the word before school's out." A few of the other guys nodded.

"OK," said Rob. "Here's what we've got so far: Donnie, you're sure your folks are going to be out of town on the thirty-first?"

"Yes."

"Then it's all set. Let's get things rolling at about 10:00 or 10:30. Jared, what are you bringing?"

"Ice and drinks—non-alcoholic, of course."

"Bor-ring!" somebody said.

"C'mon, guys," Rob said with a phony grin, "we're in basketball season, remember? Alcohol's a no-no." His friends laughed. "OK, Donnie," he continued, "you're arranging the munchies, right?"

"No problem."

"And I've got the tunes," said Rob as the bell rang. "Let everybody know: Donnie Becker's house, New Year's Eve, 10:00." The group broke up as the rush to fifth period began.

"What are you guys up to?" Leisel asked as she joined them.

"We got a New Year's party in the works," said Rob. "Want to come?"

"Depends. I'm not going if you're going to act like a jerk again."

"Me? Since when have I acted like a jerk?"

"Don't answer that, Leisel," said Jared. "We don't have enough time to list all his stupid stunts."

"Cute, guys, real cute," said Rob. "Look, you ought to come, Leisel.

It'll be cool. There'll be food, fun, tunes, and some fizzy stuff to drink. Me and Jared'll pick you up."

"*You* I can trust," she said to Jared as she looped her arm around his waist. "Is this going to be a decent party?"

"Probably not," Jared answered, "if Rob's going to be there and provide *his* music. But if you bring earplugs, it'll be tolerable. But I promise if—" Jared was interrupted by a not-so-friendly jab in the back. He spun around to see who did it.

"Still hanging out with the Momos, eh?" Sam Boggs, reeking of marijuana, leered at Jared. "When you gonna wise up, dude? These people," he pointed at Leisel, "are evil. It's a cult religion."

"What's your problem, Boggs?" asked Rob.

Boggs smacked a pamphlet against his palm. "I been reading some real interesting stuff here 'bout the Mormon cult. *Real* interesting stuff. Says here, Jared," he smacked the pamphlet again, "that these guys'll brainwash you and before you know it, you'll be one of them. They use their women as bait, you know, to lure dumb dudes like you into their cult."

Leisel stepped forward, bristling mad. "*Bait?* You're an idiot, Sam. Come on, guys," she pulled on Jared's and Rob's arms, "let's get out of here before I drop-kick Boggs."

"Sounds like a good idea," Jared said. "I'll hold him."

Boggs dodged Jared. "See, and they're violent too." When he was out of kicking range, he called to Jared, "But I still have some hope for you as long as you're hanging out with my man Whitman. He's not a regular Momo like the rest of them—he knows how to party." Boggs disappeared into the crowd heading for class.

Leisel scowled but said nothing.

"Regular Mormon?" joked Jared. "Do you guys come in premium too?"

Rob didn't laugh. "Forget it," he said as he turned to go to his locker. "The guy's a jerk."

Leisel pulled Jared in the direction of her locker. "I hate that kind of stuff," she said.

"No doubt about it, Boggs is sewer slime."

"That's not what I meant. I mean I hate anti-Mormon garbage. You saw that pamphlet he was waving around?"

Jared nodded and was pretty sure he knew where it had been printed. His stomach twisted into a knot. Now when things were just starting to go well between them, he didn't want her to find out his dad was a hate peddler.

"What kind of creep would print garbage like that?" she asked.

"Some people are just full of hate, I guess. Maybe they have some kind of weird mental disorder or something."

"It makes me so mad." Leisel stopped in front of her locker. "I can't understand why people would read or write that stuff. Doesn't it make you *mad*?" She pushed the overflowing books and papers back into her locker, slammed it shut, and turned to face Jared.

"Believe me, I hate that stuff even more than you do," he said.

"So you don't hate Mormons?"

"No."

"Do you hate me?" She smiled and leaned into him so he had to put one arm around her shoulder to support her.

"Uh, hate's not exactly the first word that comes to mind when I think of you." He tried to look studious. "No, I can definitely say that I don't hate you. More like," he gulped, "more like just the opposite."

"Really?" Leisel beamed again, that same smile that Jared had come to love. "I'm glad."

Right then he wanted to wrap his arms around her but didn't dare. With one arm still around her shoulder, he pushed her gently in the direction of the hall door. "You'd better go, or we'll both be late to class."

Leisel turned to leave but held Jared's hand a moment longer. "Call me tonight, will you?" She waved and hurried down the hallway, her white Nikes squeaking as she went.

———————

Boggs met Jared in front of the locker room door before basketball practice that afternoon.

"You must be lost, Boggs," said Jared. "This area is for athletes, people who exercise and work. You're risking your reputation hanging around here."

"Want to talk to you, man." Boggs grinned slyly and motioned Jared to follow him around the corner of the building.

"Forget it. I'm already late."

"It's important, Hills."

"From you?" Jared laughed. "Listen, I don't do drugs." He turned to leave.

"Ever hear of Klannton Press?" Boggs held up a wad of pamphlets.

Jared froze.

"Thought you might have. I met your old man a couple days ago, Jared. Nice guy, though he and I don't see eye-to-eye on hairstyles, music, and, what shall I say—recreational habits?—but we do think alike about race and religion. He's paying me eight bucks an hour to deliver some of his stuff—real interesting stuff, by the way. You read it?"

"You're a jerk."

Boggs smirked. "Let's not get nasty. I just wanted to let you know that you and me, we got lots more in common than I ever thought. My dad is regular pals with your dad. They been going to meetings together for almost two years now and just last week made the connection that they got sons at the same school."

"Look," Jared spoke slowly, "I don't like you. I don't like how you look, I don't like what you do, and I especially don't like how you think. Why don't you just leave now before I rub your face into the wall?"

"Cool it, dude. I just wanted to let you know that I *understand*. I see where you're coming from now. Your old man's got you infiltrating the cult so you can disrupt it, right? Hey, it's cool."

Jared dropped his duffle bag and shoved Boggs against the wall. "You make me sick. Those guys are my friends." Jared pushed harder. "And their enemies are *my* enemies." He turned Boggs loose and picked up his duffle bag to go to practice.

"Whoa, I had you all wrong, man. They've already got you brainwashed, don't they? Does your old man know?"

Jared spun around, his eyes flashing. "You tell him, Boggs, and I'll—"

"Tell him? Truth is, I haven't decided who to tell what, my friend. Your old man, that might be interesting. If he's anything like my dad, he'd probably throw you around the house a little bit before throwing you out. But I thought your buddies, Leisel and Rob, might like to know about your family business."

"No!"

Boggs smiled. "I'll keep you in suspense for a while. And now I think you'd better hurry up and get into your jock rags for practice. See you around, Hills."

Jared stood at the side of the building and watched Boggs walk across the parking lot. Anger and frustration made his eyes well with tears as he thought about his dad and his friends and especially about Leisel, and how Boggs—stupid Sam Boggs—was going to ruin everything.

chapter 7

The frigid air of the winter night settled on the apartment like fog. Jared had collapsed into his *futon* and wriggled under the heavy quilts, waiting for sleep to carry him away. A couple of hours later, his nightmare again jolted him awake.

"No!" he shouted between sleep and waking.

For a few seconds he sat on his *futon,* peering into the darkness. He heard some shuffling on the other side of the room and saw a dark figure moving to the wall. In a moment, the overhead light snapped on, and Elder Newcomb stood in his white cotton pajamas blinking at Jared.

"I, uh, heard something, heard you. Are you OK?"

Jared dropped back onto his *futon* and covered his eyes with his arm. "Yeah. Just a bad dream, a nightmare."

"Really?" Newcomb rubbed his eyes with his fist and yawned. "I used to have those all the time. When I was thirteen or fourteen, I always had the same dream that I was trapped in the school library and the bookshelves were closing in on me, blocking me in. And the whole time, the bell was ringing for the next class, but I couldn't get out. Then I'd panic because, well, I'm normally a very punctual person, and . . ." He saw that

Jared wasn't listening. "Well, anyway, Mom always told me not to pressure myself so much. Every time I woke up with a nightmare, she'd make me some warm milk mixed with a little sugar, and that really helped me get to sleep. 'Course," he tapped his teeth, "that stuff ruined my teeth, but it's not Mom's fault."

"Go to sleep, Elder."

Newcomb looked at his calculator wristwatch. "My heck, it's two A.M." He flipped off the switch and padded over to his *futon*. "Good night, Elder."

Jared concentrated on his breathing to calm himself back to sleep, to clear his head of the nightmare. He was nearly asleep when Newcomb's voice floated across the room.

"You asleep?"

Jared pretended not to hear.

"Are you asleep?" This time his voice was a little louder.

"Elder," said Jared, "it's two in the morning. I'm *supposed* to be asleep."

"Sorry, but I can't sleep. Maybe it's delayed jet lag or something, but I'm wide awake."

"Well, fight it." Jared turned over and pulled the quilts tighter around himself. The room was quiet for a minute.

"Do me a favor?"

"Huh?"

"A favor." Newcomb paused. "After the milk, Mom always told me a story, something simple. I was wondering . . ."

"Give me a break, for crying out loud."

"Well, you never finished telling me about Alicia, you know, how she got you interested in the Church and all."

"It's after two in the *morning*."

"Please?"

By this time, Jared was wide awake too, so he gave in, sat up on his *futon* and pulled the quilts around his knees. "I can't believe this." He took a deep breath, pushed back his hair and thought for a moment. "OK, Leisel—"

"Oh, yeah, that's her name."

"Leisel and I were kind of going together, I guess. I'd go around to her house sometimes and I got to know her family pretty well. Before everything fell apart I used to even go over for Sunday dinner when my dad was out of town." He pulled his knees forward, rested his chin on them and sighed. Good memories. "Her family was the greatest. Really, I think they had as much to do with me getting interested in the Church as she did."

*   *   *   *   *

Christmas vacation and a girlfriend. Jared had never had a regular girlfriend before, and now that he had one, he was looking forward to having two weeks of free time to spend with her.

His dad made him work weekday mornings in the print shop so he had afternoons off for basketball practice. The rest of his time he planned on spending with Leisel Lee.

The first Tuesday evening of vacation, they planned to go Christmas shopping together. Jared showed up at Leisel's house, a large brick home.

Her father answered the door. "Well, merry Christmas, Jared." He shook Jared's hand and pulled him into the house with one motion. "It's good to see you again. Come on in. Leisel's still upstairs getting ready."

Jared followed him into the living room and sat down.

"So, what are you two doing tonight?"

"A little Christmas shopping, I guess."

"Oh, that's right. Leisel's been complaining that I haven't taken her yet. I've just been so busy at work that I haven't even had a chance to . . ." Mr. Lee grimaced. "Rats, that reminds me. I still haven't figured out what I'm going to get for my wife. She's murder about birthday and Christmas presents. It's almost impossible for me to get her something and keep it secret. She usually knows when I'm out shopping, and even if I do manage to get away without her knowing, one of the kids blabs. Sometimes I think she gets more pleasure out of guessing what I've gotten her than she does from the gift itself." He looked at Jared and smiled. "I bet it's the same way around your house."

"Well, not exactly. My dad's not real big on getting presents for us. If he ever did get Mom anything at all, it'd be a huge surprise. He usually just gives me some money and tells me to get her something."

Mr. Lee's face lit up. "You know, that might work for me." He looked in the direction of the kitchen. "Betty, you still in there?" He waited for a second to make sure she was gone, then lowered his voice. "I think she's upstairs supervising the little kids' baths. Listen, Jared, why don't I give you and Leisel some money tonight and have you buy my wife's present for me? Leisel knows what she likes and it'll drive Betty crazy to think I haven't gone shopping. What do you say?"

"Yeah, sure. We'll be glad to."

"That'd be great," Mr. Lee said, pulling a couple twenty-dollar bills from his wallet and handing them to Jared. "I really appreciate it."

Just then, Leisel's little brothers—three blond-haired boys dressed in pajamas with their wet hair slicked back—came flying down the stairs and into the living room.

"Hey, Jared!" said Enoch, the five year old, as he dove into his lap. Jared stood up and with his free arm caught Danny, the seven year old, as he jumped at him. The three of them tumbled back onto the sofa.

"Boys," said Mr. Lee, "if you hurt Jared, he won't want to come over here anymore."

Nathan, the oldest boy at nine, landed next to Jared on the sofa. "No way, Dad. Jared'll keep coming over because he likes Leisel."

"Ew, gross!" Enoch stuck out his tongue and made a face.

"Yuck," said Danny. "You don't really *like* girls, do you? At my school all they do is chase me at recess and cry when I hit them to make them stop.

"And you know what," continued Danny, giggling, "on TV, I saw this man and this girl kissing, right on the mouth, and then they fell onto their bed and were wrestling and stuff, getting all tangled up in the blankets and—"

"Sick!" said Enoch, looking like he'd just swallowed a mouthful of fish eggs. "I'm never going to kiss any stupid old girl."

"Bet you will," said Nathan. "When he gets older, huh, Jared? You bet he'll kiss a girl."

Jared smiled at Enoch. "Yes. He'll probably have girls begging him to kiss them."

Enoch sat up straight. "Will not. Will not. Yuck!" He dragged his arm across his mouth.

"Some girls aren't so bad," said Nathan.

"Nathan has a girlfriend, Nathan has a girlfriend," laughed Danny as he bounced on the sofa.

"Do not!" Nathan punched his brother in the arm. "It's just that I'm older, like Jared, and older guys know about girls more. Right, Jared?"

"Yeah, well, I suppose it does change when you get older, maybe about the time when girls stop chasing you at recess."

Enoch grabbed Jared by the cheeks and drew his face close to his. "You don't kiss my stupid sister, do you?"

"That's enough, boys," said Mr. Lee. "Give the poor guy some privacy. Someday you boys'll learn that gentlemen never kiss and tell."

"What's that supposed to mean?" asked Danny.

"I'll explain it to you when you get older," said Mr. Lee. "Now you guys get upstairs and get ready for bed. And while you're up there, tell Leisel Jared's down here waiting."

Enoch slid off Jared's lap and to the floor, puckering his face up as he did. "Girls, yech. I'm going to go brush my teeth."

"Hey, Leisel," called Danny as he stomped up the stairs making loud smooching sounds, "your boyfriend's here."

Leisel came downstairs a few minutes later followed by her younger sister, Michelle.

"What was going on down here?" asked Leisel as she sat next to Jared. "Danny and Enoch are up in the bathroom giggling and making kissing sounds, trying to gross each other out."

"Kissing yucky girls," said Mr. Lee. "The boys were discussing all the gross things related to romance. Your name came up."

A blush of bright pink grew at the base of Leisel's throat, but she smiled at her dad. "I knew I should have drowned them in the bathtub when they were still little. Now they're going to spend their youth embarrassing me all the time."

"What about me?" asked Michelle. At thirteen, she was starting to become more concerned about what boys thought of her. "Daddy, if you let them act that way around Leisel's boyfriends, it's going to be even worse for me."

"They're just being boys," Mr. Lee laughed. "I used to do the same thing to my sisters."

"But it's not funny, and we're not living in the pioneer days. I swear, Daddy, if they ever do that to the boys who come over to see me . . ."

"Wait a minute," he answered, still grinning, "you better not have boys over here any time soon."

"I know." Michelle paused a moment. "But, well, OK, but it's just not polite."

"I'll tell you what," he said, finally looking more serious. "I'll talk to them about it. I've got to go upstairs and help Mom put them to bed now anyway." He stood and started up the stairs. "Guess *I'll* have to be the one to tease the boys."

"He makes me so mad sometimes," Michelle muttered after he was gone.

"Don't worry about him," said Leisel. "He's just being a father."

A father, thought Jared. *What would it be like to have a father like that?*

"Hey, Jared, you still with us?" Leisel shook his arm. "Don't zone out on me now; you've got to drive to the mall."

"Huh? Oh, sorry. I was just thinking."

"For a minute there, I was afraid my little brothers inflicted brain damage or something. You ready?"

"Don't know. After all that deep talk about yucky girls, I'm not sure if I still want to go with you or not. Promise you won't chase me at recess?"

Leisel poked him in the ribs. "Don't start talking like Enoch." She pulled Jared to his feet. "You don't mind if Michelle comes too, do you? I made her promise not to be too much of a pain." Michelle stood behind her, batting her eyes at Jared.

Actually, he did mind. "No, I guess not."

"Mom's idea," explained Leisel as they headed for the door with Michelle trailing behind them. "She still doesn't trust you."

"Do you?"

Leisel smiled and squeezed his hand. "I haven't decided yet, so you better watch yourself."

"Hey, Jared!" Enoch caught up with them before they were out the door. One toe poked through the blue foot of his Spider-Man pajamas and a white ring of toothpaste lined his mouth. "I forgot to ask you if you wanna go to church with me Sunday. Dad said it's OK."

"He won't want to go with you, stupid," said Michelle. "He's Leisel's friend."

"Yeah, but he's my friend too, huh, Jared?"

"You bet, bud. I like all of you guys. Sure, if I can, I'll be glad to go to church with you on Sunday. You all go together, don't you?"

Enoch nodded. "But I want you to sit by me."

"No problem. Just have to make sure it's OK with my mom and dad first."

"How come?" Enoch scrunched up his nose. "Maybe they won't want you to sit by me?"

"No, see, they belong to a different church, and . . ."

"They aren't Mormons?"

"Nope."

"Are you?" Enoch looked like he was trying to figure out a puzzle.

"Afraid not."

"How come?" He peered up into Jared's face. Leisel looked at him too, as if to ask the same question.

"Stop being a pest," interrupted Michelle. "That's none of your business. Now get up to bed."

Enoch dodged Michelle's grasp and turned to go upstairs. "'S OK, Jared. You can still come to our church. See you."

———————

On the way to the mall, Jared told Leisel and Michelle about their father's plan to have them buy their mom's present. The three of them sat in the front seat talking about Sister Lee and what she'd like for Christmas, Leisel suggesting one thing, Michelle rejecting it and suggesting something else. It was warm in the car; Christmas music played on the radio, and Jared, driving to the mall with two sisters, felt like part of a family, at least what he thought a family should feel like.

———————

At the mall, Leisel took charge. Jared could barely keep up with her as she led them from one store to another in search of the perfect Christmas gift for their mother.

"If there's one thing I know, it's shopping," she said as she steered Jared and Michelle through the mall crowd. "But this is a special challenge. The trick is to find something that would be typical Dad and still be something Mom will like."

They walked past a chocolate specialty store and Michelle stopped. "Hey, what about some candy? I love chocolate."

"We're shopping for Mom, not for you," said Leisel. Then she stopped and pointed to a nearby music store. "But wait a minute. Let me take a look in there."

She pushed through the crowd and into the store while Jared and Michelle went into the candy store, bought a bag of chocolate-covered almonds, and sat on a bench in front of the store.

"Leisel's a pretty serious shopper."

"Pretty serious everything," said Michelle. "She's really got this thing about doing stuff right. Well, almost everything."

"Almost?"

"Yeah. Dad says the only thing keeping her from being translated is her bedroom. He won't even go in there anymore because it's such a pit. You ever notice how she almost always wears the same running shoes?"

He hadn't ever really thought about it, but, yes, he had noticed that Leisel usually wore a pair of white Nikes.

"Well, that's because she can never find the mates to any of her other shoes or sandals. They're all somewhere around the house, but she likes to kick them off one at a time. One might be in the family room under the couch, another might be outside. There's probably a bunch in her room, but the carpet in there hasn't seen daylight since she was fourteen and Grandma Lee came to visit and stayed in Leisel's room."

Jared laughed.

"It drives Daddy crazy, so he refuses to buy her any new shoes until she can show him a complete pair that is either worn out or too small. For the last three Sundays, she's had to wear a pair of Mom's old high heels to church."

"Thanks, Michelle," Jared laughed. "Now I know what to get her for Christmas."

"I know what she got you."

"Oh, yeah? A pair of shoes?"

"She'd kill me if I told you. All I can say is that she spent a fortune, all the money she had saved to buy herself a new pair of shoes. She really likes you."

Jared didn't know what to say.

"Leisel says you guys have been to the Mesa Temple Visitors' Center. How'd you like it?"

Jared liked it. Leisel had talked him into going there a couple times since they started going out. The workers at the center were all old but friendly, and when he was there in the shadow of the Mesa Temple, he felt a sense of peace that made him want to learn more about Leisel's church.

The only trouble was his dad. The last time he was in the center, he noticed a rack of pamphlets near the exit and for a moment stopped to look at them, afraid that they might have been planted there by his dad.

"Interested in any of these?" asked an elderly man. "They're free."

Jared declined, but he was glad to see that someone was printing something good about the Mormons.

"You know what else?" Michelle popped the last piece of candy into her mouth and crumpled the bag. "My whole family likes you. The boys think you're cool, and even Dad and Mom think you're OK." She looked down shyly. "And I think you're OK too." Her face turned bright red.

"Well, you guys are a great family. And you're like the little sister I never had."

Michelle looked up surprised, then smiled.

Finally, Leisel came out of the music store with a bright yellow bag. "I found the perfect gifts, guys. Remember how Mom said she met Dad?"

"At a play or something at BYU?" said Michelle.

"Right, *South Pacific*. And you know how Dad loves to sing that really corny song, 'Some Enchanted Evening'? Well, I bought the original soundtrack and one of those karaoke sing-along CDs. Next we'll go down to the video store and buy the movie. Dad can give it all to Mom with a special note inside."

Jared and Michelle followed Leisel as she continued to explain her idea on the way to the DVD shop. "Dad can buy her a dozen roses, you and I can prepare a really fancy tropical dinner for them and then take the boys to McDonald's and leave them alone for 'Some Enchanted Evening.' And after the movie, Dad can even sing her a love song if he wants.

"What do you guys think?" Leisel glowed.

"Romantic," said Michelle. "Mom'll love it."

"Sounds better than a bottle of perfume," Jared said. And as he watched Leisel walk through the crowd, her long blonde hair bouncing behind her, he noticed her white running shoes. He'd definitely get her a pair of shoes, and he decided he'd also better get her something romantic to go with them. What, he didn't know.

On the way home, Leisel wanted to stop by the temple's visitors' center. "You've got to see the Christmas lights, Jared. They're really incredible."

The night air was cool and dry, but the temple grounds glowed warmly in the white and yellow light. Strings of tiny white lights filled the trees and shrubs all around the visitors' center, and as they neared the center, they could hear the faint strains of a quartet singing Christmas carols in the area behind the main building.

As they joined the crowd of listeners, Leisel held Jared's arm and leaned into him. "I love this place at Christmastime. It's exactly what I need to put me in the mood for the holidays. Remember, Michelle, how Dad used to bring us here every year for the first home evening in December? That's when he'd always drill into us that Christmas is a time to think of Christ, love, and our family, not of what gifts we'd get."

"Yeah," said Michelle, "and I always used to think he was just using that as an excuse not to buy us many presents."

"Someday," Leisel said, "after I get married in there," she pointed to the temple, "I'm going to bring my kids here and let them feel the spirit of Christmas, too. Don't you think this is what Christmas should feel like?" Leisel's eyes sparkled.

Jared agreed, and as he watched her, he was struck with how happy she looked: pure and simple happiness. He realized that she had something he didn't, something he wanted to have too.

They stayed until the concert was over, and on the way home, Jared decided it was time to do something about this feeling he had when he was around Leisel and her family.

"You know, I'm pretty sure I'll be able to come to church with you guys on Sunday. Be sure and tell Enoch for me, OK?"

"All right!" said Michelle. "Maybe you can stay for dinner after, huh?"

Jared nodded. "And there's something else." He swallowed and tried not to think of the blowup this would cause with his dad. "I've been thinking, you know, about your church and everything. Lots of it seems to make sense."

"Of course it makes sense," Leisel said. "I've been telling you that for weeks."

"Well, I was wondering if Sunday your dad or somebody could tell me more about it. Maybe they can give me some stuff to read or something."

"Oh, Jared, that's wonderful! I can't believe this! Where do you want to talk to them? They can go over to your house if you want."

Jared knew the explosion that would trigger and said, "That wouldn't be a good idea. My dad's got this thing about Mormons. Could we talk at your church or some other place?"

"You can use our house. I'm sure Mom and Dad would love that!"

"OK, then, it's set," Jared said as he pulled his car into their driveway.

Leisel stayed in the front seat a moment after Michelle got out and ran into the house, eager to tell her parents about Jared's request. "I can't even tell you how excited I am. I mean, I didn't think, well I was hoping and stuff, but . . . this is the best Christmas present ever." She threw her arms around him, kissed him, then slid across the seat and out the door. "Good night, Jared." Her eyes glistened with tears. "Thanks for everything."

Jared took his time driving home and swung by the temple one more time to look at it. He had a good feeling about what was happening with his life and with Leisel. He looked forward to Sunday and just hoped that his dad wouldn't find out. He knew that if he did, his dream would turn into a nightmare.

chapter 8

Jared awoke to the sound of rattling pans and running water in the kitchen. Last night's story hadn't ended until nearly 3:00 and it wasn't until he finished it that he realized his companion was already sleeping, snoring softly in his *futon* on the other side of the room. Oh well.

He was a little irritated for having stayed up telling Newcomb a bedtime story, but he had enjoyed recalling the times with the Lees. Without them, he wouldn't be here. Without Leisel—well, he didn't want to think about that just now.

He threw his quilt back and the cold December air stung him, making him shiver as he walked into the kitchen to grab his scriptures and greet his companion. From the kitchen doorway, he saw Newcomb, already dressed for the day, whistling a Christmas carol off-key as he stirred a pot of boiling *mugi* on their gas stove.

"*Ohaiyo,* Elder!" Newcomb said cheerfully. "I used the mission home recipe book to prepare breakfast. I figured it was my turn, and after last night, I thought you might be kind of tired." He smiled and pushed his glasses back up the bridge of his nose. His hair was slicked back and he wore a light blue, full-length apron that had "Le Chef" written across it in red cursive. "By the time you're done with scriptures, I should have everything ready. Toast and eggs go OK with *mugi*?"

"Nothing goes OK with *mugi*," Jared replied, "but toast and eggs sound great." He smiled and gave him the thumbs-up sign. "Thanks, Elder," he said before he walked back to his room to read. *Newcomb's a little strange,* he thought as he opened his Book of Mormon, *and he is a real wimp, but he's OK. Might even be a good companion.*

————————

"I wish we had a red tablecloth or something," said Newcomb as he dabbed his toast into the yolk of his egg. "Mom always used a red table-cloth in December to make things Christmassy. And we had a Santa Claus silverware set that we'd use the whole month."

"Santa Claus silverware?"

"You know, the forks had Santa shapes and the spoons had reindeer shapes on the handles."

"And *you* used these?"

"Just in December. See, Mom liked to make it special for us kids . . ."

"Santa silverware? Come on, Elder, you weren't actually using that stuff last year?"

"Yeah, sure, they were my favorite," he paused and then blushed when he realized Jared was laughing at him. "Oh, well, I mean, when I was a *kid* they were my favorite. Just Christmas memories, know what I mean?"

Jared nodded.

"What'd your family do special for Christmas?"

"Not a heck of a lot. Practically nothing. My dad wasn't much into the holiday spirit."

Newcomb looked sad. "So you don't have any good Christmas memories?"

"Oh, I've got some. One in particular, I guess, but it wasn't with my family. My dad almost ruined it."

"Was it with Crystal's family?"

"*Leisel*'s family. Yeah, it was with them."

*   *   *   *   *

Church wasn't anything like Jared had expected. No candles, no incense burning, no deep, dark formality. He felt self-conscious at first—several kids he recognized from school were there—but once the meeting started, he felt comfortable.

He sat with the Lee family, Leisel on one side, Enoch scrunched next to him on the other. It was the Sunday before Christmas and Rob's dad, Bishop Whitman, conducted the meeting. A kid Jared's age spoke first, then the ward choir sang several Christmas carols, then Bishop Whitman spoke about Christmas. That was the part Jared liked best.

"In today's world," said the bishop, "there are plenty of problems: war, hatred, disease, famine, crime. Perhaps some of these modern-day plagues have touched you personally; you certainly know of people who have been affected by these ills. But this time of year we pause to celebrate the birth of Jesus Christ, a time when the angels told us to celebrate 'peace on earth.'

"Life's not easy in these times, but the Lord has promised us his peace. That doesn't mean we won't have problems; it doesn't even mean that we'll always be happy. But accepting the gospel of Jesus Christ and living its teachings means that we're guaranteed some peace and happiness in this life and perfect peace and happiness in the life to come."

Peace and happiness in this life and the life to come. That's what Jared wanted and that's what he usually found when he was around Leisel's family. He looked down the row: Enoch had fallen asleep with his head resting in Jared's lap. Danny and Nathan, in white shirts and ties, sat next to their mom. Michelle sat on the other side of her father with her arm around him. For a moment, Jared almost felt a part of this wonderful family.

This, he thought, *is what I want.*

"Christmas," continued Bishop Whitman, "is a time for us to share the peace and joy that we have. Just as Christ's family shared their peace and happiness with the shepherds and angels around Bethlehem, we should do what we can to share our blessings with those around us."

———————

After church, the missionaries and Jared had dinner together at the Lee's house. And after dinner, the missionaries met with Jared in the living room. Leisel sat next to him on the sofa, holding his hand most of the time, while the elders explained to Jared about the First Vision and the restoration of the gospel.

Jared had never experienced a feeling like he had with the missionaries. He knew, even as they spoke, that what they were telling him was true. He realized that he still had a lot to learn, but something inside him told him that this was it; this was what would guarantee him true joy.

"So, Jared," said one of the elders as they completed their presentation, "if you pray about this and are convinced it's true, would you be willing to be baptized?"

Jared thought of his father, of what he would do or say if Jared joined the Church. It scared him, but then he remembered Bishop Whitman's talk and the warm secure feeling he had in sacrament meeting. He knew he would have to make a decision sooner or later and no matter when he did it, choosing the gospel would make big trouble at home.

"Things are kind of tricky with my parents and all," he said. "I'd have to talk to them first, kind of explain to them."

The missionaries nodded.

"And it couldn't be right away. I mean, it will take some time for me to figure all this out and then figure out how to let my dad know." He looked at Leisel and squeezed her hand before going on. "But I already know it's true, I guess. I mean, I believe everything you've told me. So, yeah, I want to be baptized. I just don't know when."

The words were barely out of Jared's mouth when Leisel threw her arms around him.

With Leisel crying in his arms, Jared didn't know what the future held for him, but he did know that he wanted Leisel and the Church to be a part of it.

———————

After the missionaries left, Leisel told her family the news. In a few minutes, her brothers stormed into the room and mobbed Jared. "So you're going to get baptized?" asked Danny. "Even before me?"

"Well, you never know. Things with my dad are sort of—"

"After you're baptized," said Enoch, "I can call you Brother Hills and you'll be like a big brother. And you'll be nice to me, not like Danny and Nathan." He crawled onto Jared's lap. "When they're being mean to me, Jared, will you beat them up?"

"No way, stupid," said Nathan as he jumped onto the sofa next to Jared. "He won't beat us up just 'cause you tell him to. He's our friend too."

Danny stood in front of Jared. "But is Enoch right? Are you going to be like our brother?"

"You guys are so dumb," said Nathan. "He's just going to be Brother Hills, a member of the Church. The only way he could ever be like a brother—a part-of-the-family brother—is if he *married* Leisel. That'd make him our brother-in-law."

Enoch's face clouded and he stuck out his lower lip. "But he'd never want to marry my dumb sister! Isn't there some other way? Huh, Jared?"

"Hold it, guys. I'm pretty sure I'll be a Mormon someday, sooner or later, but I don't know about marrying your sister. I mean, we're still awful young, and she'll probably have millions of guys wanting to marry her."

"I'll beat them all up." Enoch held out a fist.

"Yeah, and I'll tell them how ugly she looks in the morning," said Danny.

The boys continued their teasing and questioning until Mr. Lee came in and chased them out. "I need to talk to Jared alone for a few minutes."

"So, Jared," he said as he lowered himself into the chair opposite him, "you're really considering baptism?"

"It seems like the right thing to do."

"What about your parents?"

Jared sighed. "That's the scary part. Mom will be OK, I think, as long as she's sure Dad won't go completely nuts. He's not exactly pro-Mormon."

"Would it help if I talked to him?"

Jared tried to imagine Mr. Lee and his dad talking about the Church. It wasn't a happy picture. "No, I don't think that would work. Dad's not exactly a great listener, and he's already got this hang-up about Mormons. I'll find some way to tell him."

"This is really none of my business, but I think you need to talk to your parents before you go any further with this. They have a right to know. You owe them that."

"Yeah, but . . ."

"I know it seems hard right now, but what's right is what's right. I'd like nothing better than to have you join the Church. You're a good kid. I like you. My kids like you. Leisel, well, I think she more than likes you. We all want what's best for you, but we don't want it at the expense of your relationship with your own family."

Jared remained silent, letting Mr. Lee's advice sink in. He knew he should talk to his parents about the Church, but it would be so much easier not to. When his dad found out, there'd be no telling what would happen. Jared could handle his dad, but he couldn't handle what his dad might do in the community, what he might do or say to the Lees or to

Leisel, or what he might do with Sam Boggs to make Jared's life miserable.

Jared sighed. "OK. I'll do what I can. I really appreciate your talking to me and all. It's been great."

As Jared stood up to leave, Mr. Lee did something Jared's father had never done. He hugged him.

"You're a great young man," he said. "We'll be praying for you."

He walked Jared to the front door and called for Leisel to let her know he was leaving. Jared thanked Mr. Lee again and walked out to his car with Leisel.

"Your dad's a good guy," he said.

"Most of the time. He really cares about you." She smiled. "We all do." She leaned over and kissed his cheek.

"Thanks for today," he said. "Thanks for everything."

———————

Christmas morning dawned cold and gloomy at Jared's house. His father had worked late the night before and came home noisy and obnoxious, but Jared had managed to avoid him. He hadn't yet found the time or the courage to talk to either of his parents about his interest in the Church, and he didn't plan on ruining his Christmas by battling with his dad.

From where he lay in his bed, he could see the present he had all prepared to give Leisel. It had cost him plenty, but he knew it would be the right one for her: one that she'd remember.

It wasn't yet seven o'clock, so Jared stretched and stayed in bed enjoying the quiet in the house and anticipating the evening he'd spend with Leisel and her family. Then he heard the doorbell ringing. And ringing. And ringing again. Then knocking, soft at first, then louder and faster. Jared sat up and pulled on a T-shirt and some gym shorts to go answer the door. He could hear his father downstairs cursing about being disturbed so early on Christmas morning. Jared hurried, desperate to get to the door ahead of his father.

Jared was halfway down the stairs when he heard the door open and his father exclaim, "What the—?"

"We wish you a merry Christmas, we wish you a merry Christmas, we wish you a merry Christmas and a Happy New Year!" It was Leisel.

"What do you want?" Jared heard the anger in his dad's voice and trotted down the rest of the stairs hoping to prevent disaster.

"You must be Mr. Hills. Merry Christmas! I'm Leisel Lee, a friend of Jared's. Is he home?"

"He's home. And you should be too. What do you think you're doing this early on a holiday?"

Jared landed at the foot of the stairs and could see his father's back stiffen as he held the door open.

"I'm sorry," Leisel's voice sounded tentative, surprised. "I just wanted to surprise him. I brought him a present. Do you think I could see him a minute? Is he up?"

"Who are you?" his father asked.

"Leisel Lee. I told Jared after church on Sunday that I might come by today. I just didn't say when."

"Church? What church?"

"My church. Didn't he tell you? I thought—"

Jared stepped forward to try to save the situation before his whole world exploded. "Leisel!" he said too cheerfully. "Hey, what are you doing here? Dad, this is Leisel, a friend from school. Geez, Leisel, I didn't think you'd come over so early." He slipped past his dad and through the door.

She looked from Jared to his father. Sensing the tension in the air, she backed up a few steps and said, "Maybe this isn't a good time."

"I asked you what church." Jared's father's stare hadn't left Leisel.

Leisel glanced at Jared, then said, "Mesa Seventeenth Ward. The LDS Church."

"Mormons." He swore. "I was afraid of this." He pushed the hair back from his forehead and exhaled slowly. "Jack Boggs told me this would happen and I just couldn't believe it. Jared," his voice cracked like a bull-whip, "you been seeing this Mormon girl?"

"Yes, sir." Jared stood between Leisel and his dad. "She's a pretty good friend of mine." He paused. "So's her family."

His father's face turned red and hard. "Thought I made it plain to you, son. This kind of garbage just won't do. Not in my house, not in my family."

"Mr. Hills," Leisel tried to step around Jared, but he held out his arm to keep her behind him, "it's really all my fault. See, I just invited him to—"

"You!" he shouted. "I don't want to hear from you. Just get back in your little car and get the hell out of my driveway, off my property. I don't want to hear your lies and I don't want you messing with my son. I got to deal with him here and now, my own way." His knuckles turned white on the door's edge.

Leisel's eyes filled with tears and her face flushed, but she didn't budge. "I'm sorry. I didn't come here to make trouble or to upset you, Mr. Hills. I just wanted to give Jared this," she held out a gift-wrapped package, "and wish him a merry Christmas."

Before Jared could grab the present, his father stepped outside and slapped it out of her hands and into the shrubs that lined the front of the house.

"I already asked you nicely to get out of here," he hissed, "now am I going to have to get ugly?"

Leisel backed away, tears flowing freely now. "What's the matter with you? You have no right. Jared, I'm sorry. I didn't mean for it to be like this." She turned and ran to her car.

Jared tried to follow her to explain, to apologize, but before he could take a step, his dad grabbed him by his T-shirt collar and yanked him back to the house.

"Stinking Mormon-lover," were the last words he remembered hearing before his world turned black.

———————

Jared woke up on the sofa in their living room with his head throbbing. Next to him sat his mother, crying softly and wiping his forehead with a cool, damp cloth. The back of his head felt like it had caved in and as he tried to move, pain shot through his skull and down his neck.

He groaned.

"I think you'll be OK," his mother said. Tears streaked her face. "I can't believe he did this. I don't know what got into him. You know you shouldn't make him mad."

Jared raised up and gingerly touched the lump on the back of his head. "What happened? Where's Dad?"

"Gone. I don't know where. I heard some shouting, and then he came running into our bedroom." She spoke rapidly without looking at Jared. "He was upset, he could hardly speak. He said he grabbed you to pull you into the house, but your heels caught on the sidewalk step. You both fell, but your head hit the front step. I helped him bring you in here, and as soon as he was sure you were OK, he left."

"I think I'm all right, Mom." His head throbbed as he turned it from side to side. "But could you get me some aspirin or something?" As she left, Jared sat up and looked around their dark and simple living room. From a radio in his parents' room, he could hear the faint strains of Christmas music.

Jared and his mother ate Christmas dinner alone that afternoon. Neither spoke much.

———————

He felt better after the aspirin and dinner and went outside to look for Leisel's present. He found it wedged between two bushes near the front door and took it upstairs to his room to open it.

Leisel had attached a homemade Christmas card with an atrocious pun: the front had a picture of Santa holding an umbrella next to his sleigh and asked the question, "Why did Santa take an umbrella with him on Christmas?" Inside the card was the answer: "Because Mrs. Claus looked outside and said, 'Looks like rain, dear.'"

She had signed the card, "Love, Leisel," and included a brief note. "Enoch wanted to give you something too, so I stuck it on top of my present. Have the merriest and the best Christmas ever." Inside the box, he found a small envelope lying atop the white packing paper with a note and a wallet-sized kindergarten picture of Enoch inside. The note, written in fat smudged pencil strokes, read:

> "Dear Jared,
>
> Thak you for being my frend. And thaks for liking my dum sister.
> Mery Crismas!
> Luv,"

Enoch had signed his name with the "n" reversed.

Smiling, Jared set the photo on his desk. Then he pulled open the tissue paper that enclosed his gift.

It was heavy for its size and the first thing Jared noticed as he pushed the paper off it was how it sparkled and glistened in the light. A thick-cut crystal frame enclosed a five-by-seven photo of him and Leisel taken at the visitors' center one evening. One of the workers there said that they looked so happy together that he just had to take their picture. The picture had them standing at the entrance with his arm around her shoulder and hers around his waist. A gust of wind had just blown a strand of her blonde hair off her shoulder.

Jared held the frame in both hands, looked at Leisel's face, and tried to remember what she had been laughing about when the worker snapped their picture. Whatever it had been, it was a happy moment, and the two of them looked great together.

Together.

He set the photograph on his desk and looked at it again. Sunlight from his window struck the frame and refracted into a sparkling rainbow of colors, framing their photo in a band of light.

———————————

Weeks earlier, the Lees had invited Jared to their Christmas dinner, but he had declined, reluctant to disrupt their family gathering. He did agree to come over later Christmas evening to have some pie and visit with the family. That's when he planned on giving Leisel his present.

Enoch opened the door. "Jared! Hey, it's Jared! Come on in; we've been waiting." Enoch grabbed his hand and pulled him into the family room.

"Well, we were beginning to think you had forgotten us," Mrs. Lee smiled from her seat at one end of the room. "Come in and sit down, Jared. Dad was just getting ready to cut the pie."

Enoch guided Jared to a seat between himself and Leisel.

"Man, am I glad you finally showed up," said Danny. "I'm starving!"

"How could you be starving when just two hours ago you ate enough turkey to feed three families?" asked Mr. Lee.

"Then I was starving for *turkey*. Now I'm starving for *pie*!"

The family laughed and teased, and Jared enjoyed both the pie and the company.

After the plates were cleared away, Enoch and Danny towed Jared back into the family room to show off their Christmas loot. Nathan followed them, and when he had a chance, as cool and nonchalantly as he could, showed off his own presents.

Jared enjoyed playing with the boys, but he wanted to be alone with Leisel to thank her for her gift, to give her his, and to apologize for his crazy father. It was getting late and Leisel's parents had asked the boys several times to get ready for bed, but they refused to go, preferring Jared's company and their new toys. He was relieved when Mr. Lee finally took charge.

"Better get up there right now, boys," said Mr. Lee, "or Santa might just come and take all your presents back."

At that, Enoch and Danny bolted up the stairs, but Nathan lagged behind. "Aw, Dad, I know who Santa really is."

"Then you better get upstairs before Santa grounds you for the rest of the vacation." Mr. Lee looked over at Michelle. "You too, kiddo."

"But, Dad," she slapped her thighs in disgust, "I'm a *teenager.*"

"OK, Miss Teenager, you can come in the kitchen with me and your mother and help us clean up."

"What about Leisel?"

"I think she's going to be busy for a while." Mr. Lee looked at Leisel and smiled. "If I'm not mistaken, I think this young man here has been waiting to give her a present."

"Oooh," Michelle groaned and marched off upstairs while her parents went into the kitchen.

Jared got up off the floor and sat next to Leisel on the sofa.

"Are you OK?" she asked. "I mean with your dad and stuff? I had no idea he'd get mad about me coming over so early. I just wanted to surprise you."

"You surprised me, all right. And my dad, too. Sorry that he acted like such a jerk this morning."

"It was my fault."

"No, you don't know Dad." Jared got up and went to the front door and returned with his backpack. "I feel really lousy about what happened this morning, and I'm really sorry you had to go through all that. But I didn't come over to talk about my dad. So, first, your present. It was the best gift I've ever had."

She looked down. "I wanted to give you something nice, something that would remind you of me, of us. And I thought the crystal, well, it has color and it's clear. I liked that."

"It's the greatest. Really. I'll always keep it." He leaned over and kissed her.

"Now, for tonight's business." Jared pulled his backpack onto his lap. "I have something in here for you." He pulled out a gift-wrapped box and placed it on Leisel's lap. "I'm afraid it's not as fancy or romantic as yours, but I hope you'll like it anyway."

Leisel tore off the wrapping paper and opened the package. "Jared, they're beautiful!" She pulled out a pair of brown oxfords. "But how did you know?"

"About your shoe problem? Michelle told me. And your mom gave me your size. I hope you'll be able to keep these together. They're a matched pair—'sole mates'—and should never be separated. Check out the bottoms."

Leisel turned the shoes over. The leather sole of the right shoe had "Jared" branded in it. The left shoe had "Leisel."

"I could kill Michelle for telling you about my shoes, but Jared, this is just a perfect gift. I promise I'll take good care of them."

"One more thing," Jared said. "Check the laces."

Dangling from the left shoe was a small gold birthstone ring.

"I know we're not engaged or anything, but I just wanted to give you something pretty that would last."

She hugged him. "This is the best Christmas present I've ever had."

A few minutes later, they went into the kitchen to help her parents finish up the dishes. Jared even had another piece of pie. When Jared left that night, he felt good, and he wanted to keep the feeling a long time.

Forever, if he could.

chapter 9

After breakfast, Elder Newcomb spent his day learning "street contacting." He and Jared stood in front of Himeji Station and tried to strike up conversations with passersby. Most brushed past, but occasionally one or two would stop.

"You from America?" the conversation usually went. "I study English. This is a pen. My name is Hiroki . . ." Jared tried to avoid getting tied up with people who just wanted to practice their English. Newcomb, though, spent most of his time talking to curious Japanese who wanted to test their English on a real live American. It was a comic scene: Newcomb trying to communicate using broken Japanese, while the Japanese person responded in broken English.

When their day was over, they tracted the neighborhoods back to their apartment, ending the day with zero contacts, zero discussions, zero investigators. Jared felt like a loser, and his companion was exhausted, but not, to Jared's surprise, discouraged.

"This isn't so bad," he said as they pulled off their coats in their apartment. "I can do this. Did you see me talking to all those people today?

And I thought my Japanese was bad. Low self-image, that's my problem. Mom always said I was too hard on myself."

Jared sat at the kitchen table, writing zeros in his missionary report log. He tossed his pencil down. "Shut up, Elder! Please, just shut up for five minutes!"

Newcomb flinched and stopped talking immediately.

"Things have been lousy here for the past couple days, in case you haven't noticed, and I'm in no mood to sit here and listen to you run at the mouth." Jared stared, fuming at his notebook while his companion sat across the room, stunned. He had his head down, and Jared saw his hunched shoulders quivering. *Great,* thought Jared, *Now I've got him crying.* He knew he needed to set things straight, to repent, so he took a deep breath, then spoke to Newcomb.

"Hey, Elder . . . hey, I'm sorry I lost it. I don't know what got into me. Maybe it's like you said, maybe I'm too hard on myself. But a few more days like these past two and *my* self-image is going straight down the tubes." Newcomb looked up and Jared smiled. "But you know, Elder, I'm glad you're so optimistic, really. It'll help offset my negative moods." He walked over and shook Newcomb's hand. "Thanks for staying positive."

Elder Newcomb grinned at the compliment. "Well, I try to be. Mom always told me that when things got really really bad to stop and think about things that could be even worse. You know, we all have choices to make and we can choose to be positive or negative. I always try to choose the positive. Besides, there's lots worse than what happened today: you could tract out a house full of *Yakuza* gangster guys, or fall off your bike in front of a bus, or have to speak in stake conference in Japanese, or you could lose your passport and have to . . ."

As Newcomb listed Bad Things That Could Happen, Jared remembered the worst thing that ever happened to him. It didn't take much effort to call up the memory; as a matter of fact, even though it had happened more than three years ago, the memory still lingered under the surface of his consciousness like a shark under water. He knew he would never forget it, but he hoped that even if the memory never faded, at least the pain would subside.

Someday.

*   *   *   *   *

On December twenty-sixth, Jared and his father sat in the living room watching a basketball game. His dad ignored Jared, focusing on the game, his cigarettes, and his beer. An unbearable tension filled the room and Jared couldn't have enjoyed the game even if he had wanted to. He put up with the awkwardness because he hoped that he might get an opportunity to tell his father about Leisel, about the Church. He had no idea, however, how he'd pull it off if he did get a chance. Should he ask for permission to continue talking to the missionaries, or should he just announce that he was going to do it, no matter what?

As it turned out, he wouldn't have to say anything. At halftime, his father spoke. "I don't know what you been doing with that girl or what she's been telling you about her church, but I want you to get one thing straight right now." His father took a long drag on his cigarette and snuffed it out in the ashtray next to his chair. "Mormons," he said, exhaling smoke from his nostrils, "are poison. Maybe you're old enough to decide what you want to do with your own life—hell, when I was your age, I was making my own decisions—but let me tell you something." His eyes narrowed and his voice turned flat and hard. "I'm not having a son of mine turn Mormon on me. Not ever."

Jared stared at his for father a few seconds, then left the room. In his own way, his father had told him where things stood. He could continue to see Leisel, could even join the Church if he wanted; it would only cost him his membership in his family. It wasn't a choice he looked forward to making, but Jared knew he'd come to that crossroads sooner or later.

Jared didn't like basketball practice during winter vacation. The gym felt cold and practices were longer than normal because, as their coach often said, "I don't want you guys coming back to school waddling like a bunch of stuffed Santa Clauses."

"OK, men, you've earned some time off," he told them after practice on December thirtieth. "Our next workout won't be until January second. But don't let yourselves get out of shape. And don't," he stared at Rob, "get into any trouble at parties. You know the training rules, right?" Everyone nodded and those behind Rob poked him in the back.

"Then get out of here," the coach slapped his clipboard on his thigh to dismiss them, "and have a good New Year's."

The team room was steamy and noisy after practice. Rob had just finished his shower and with a towel wrapped around his waist, stood up on a bench to talk to his teammates. "OK, guys—hey, muzzle that stereo a minute, will you?—guys, don't forget our little New Year's Eve party. Becker says his house is still clear, so plan on getting there around 10:00. Any questions, children?" Rob looked over the room, then pointed at the stereo. "No? Then crank that baby back up!"

He hopped off the bench and sat next to Jared. "Man, am I looking forward to some time off. I never thought I could get tired of basketball. Hey, you're coming to the party, aren't you?"

"No wheels. My dad's been pretty ticked at me lately. Besides, I don't know if Leisel wants to go."

"She said she'd go, remember? Look, I'll drive." He nudged Jared. "What do you say?"

Jared felt torn. He enjoyed being with his teammates, but he had also thought about spending a quiet evening with Leisel. He decided he could probably do both. "Yeah," he said. "On one condition."

"Name it."

"You give me a ride home now."

90

"Saw you at church last week," Rob said as he steered his car out of the parking lot. "What'd you think?"

"It was OK. Your dad gave a good talk."

"Yeah. He's good at talks." He glanced sideways at Jared. "You and Leisel still going out?"

"We don't go out much, but I'm over at her place a lot. She's got a cool family." Jared paused. "Did you hear that I talked to the missionaries?"

"Dad said something about it. You're not thinking of turning Mormon, are you?"

"Maybe. Home life is totally insane right now and getting baptized would only make things worse. But the more I hear about it, the more sense it makes, you know?"

"It's different for me," Rob said. "I haven't really thought much about it, but one of these days I'll get serious, I guess, and work on getting a real testimony. I figure that when I'm out of high school, I can sit down and decide if I want to buy into all that—you know about missions?"

Jared nodded.

"My dad expects me to go on one. Maybe I will, but I've got to decide if this Mormon stuff is just a lifestyle or a religion. You'll be a good Mormon, but sooner or later I'll just have to do what you're doing: figure out if it's for me."

"Well, if I can find a way to get baptized without getting killed, I'll probably go for it."

"Good. The Church will be great for you. And for me too, eventually. But I need to have a little fun first, need to see what I'll be missing once I straighten up and get serious about life. After I graduate, I'll have time to start being a real Mormon and get ready for a mission and all that stuff."

Jared didn't know what to say.

Rob pulled up in front of Jared's house. "Like I said, you'll make a good Mormon. Heck," he laughed, "you're probably already a better one than I am."

———————

The next night, Rob picked up Jared and the two of them drove to Leisel's house to take her to the party.

"Hey, nice shoes," Jared said as he got out of the car to let her get in. "I'm glad to see they're still together."

Leisel giggled. "They're *sole* mates, remember? Can't be separated."

"Come on, come on," said Rob. "Get in and quit slobbering over each other."

Leisel got into the front seat; Jared closed her door, and got in back.

"What's this stuff about soul mates?" asked Rob.

"My Christmas present from Jared," said Leisel. "New shoes."

"What, Jared, you into designer shoes now?"

"No, dummy," said Leisel. "One shoe has 'Jared' written on the bottom; the other says 'Leisel.' He called them sole mates. Romantic, huh?"

"Oh, yeah," said Rob, "*real* romantic. That Jared," Rob's voice went higher, "he's just so sweet. And so original. Next time I have a girlfriend named Nike, I'll know exactly what to give her."

"Real funny, Robert." Leisel tried to look offended, but she couldn't help smiling. "OK, now about tonight: Dad says home by 1:00 A.M. or I'm grounded until I'm twenty-five."

"No sweat," said Rob. "But we better hurry so you can enjoy the total party." He turned onto the freeway entrance and accelerated.

The little Honda sped down the ramp and they could feel the acceleration nudge them deeper into their seats.

Leisel looked nervous. "Hey, Rob," she said, "slow down, will you?"

"Slow down?" Rob swerved around one car and moved into the far left lane. "What, you don't trust my driving? Jared's been cruising around with me for months, and he's still alive."

"Barely," Jared said.

"Well, I wish you'd slow down," Leisel said.

"OK, OK, here comes slow." Rob grinned and stomped on the accelerator. The Honda shot between two cars and into the right lane before slowing down for the exit ramp. "We're almost at Becker's anyway."

Jared shook his head. "You know you're going to get nailed one of these days."

"Won't happen. Besides, this car was made to go fast."

"Well, I wasn't," said Leisel. "And you know I hate it when you drive like that."

"What is this, traffic court? Look, I promise I'll drive the speed limit all the way to Becker's house."

They entered Becker's house without knocking and found Donnie in the kitchen filling bowls with party snacks. The rest of the house, a red brick split-level with a large family room downstairs, appeared empty.

"Hey, Beck," Rob said. "I got the music right here," he held up a plastic CD case. "Where's the stereo?"

"Downstairs. Go ahead and get some music going, OK? Jared, set that ice chest over here on the table."

Jared lugged his ice chest over to the table, and he and Leisel sat down to sample the chips and dip. Rob, meanwhile, bounded down the stairs; moments later, heavy guitar music echoed up the stairs.

Leisel made a face. "Is he going to play that stuff all night?"

"You know Rob," Jared said, "he loves that junk."

Donnie opened the ice chest and held up a can of soda. "I was afraid you were serious. How can you expect us to party with this kind of stuff? Good thing I was prepared."

He went to the refrigerator and pulled out two twelve-packs of beer. "We'll just mix a few of these in here with the kiddie drinks so the mature party people will have something to drink." He pulled a can out and offered it to Leisel. "You ready for one?"

"No thanks. I'm trying to quit," she said with a fake smile.

"I'd offer one to you," Donnie said to Jared, "but I know you're in training."

"So are you."

"Not until January second. And besides, it's just beer. Nobody's going to get wild on a few cans of beer."

————————

When people arrived at Becker's house, Rob acted as the official greeter, letting them in the door and directing them downstairs. Someone cranked up the music even louder and the house pulsed with the beat of a major party.

Jared and Leisel stayed in the kitchen, enjoying each other's company and helping keep the food flowing downstairs. An hour into the party Rob joined them in the kitchen. His face was flushed. "Great party, huh?"

"I'm having a blast," said Jared, "sitting here drinking 7-Up with a gorgeous Molly Mormon."

Leisel tossed a piece of ice at him. "Watch who you're calling names, Jared Gentile."

"Don't you mean Jared *Gentle*?" He put an arm around her.

"You two are getting disgusting," Rob said. "I'll just head back downstairs so I won't interrupt you two sweet soul mates."

Before Rob could leave, five guys dressed in black showed up.

"Whitman, my man!" Sam Boggs and four of his druggie buddies walked into the kitchen. "Hey, we just found out about the party. Thought we'd check it out." Boggs grinned at Jared. "And here's Jared and the Momo girl. What a sweet couple."

"Get lost, Boggs," Jared said.

"And miss the party? Dude, you know me and my buddies love parties." He looked into the open ice chest. "Only there doesn't seem to be enough party supplies for everyone. What's the deal, Rob? You already drink it all yourself?"

"Funny," said Rob. "Real funny. Look, why don't you guys get out of here before my teammates come up here and bounce you all into the street."

"Be cool, Robert. We don't plan on staying if you don't want us to. But before I go, I just want to get one thing off my chest, just wanna start my new year right, know what I mean?" He put an arm around Rob and pulled him close. "Gotta tell you something, man. Something pretty heavy."

Jared tried to think of a way to get Leisel out of the room, away from Boggs, or of a way to shut Boggs up, but things were happening too fast.

"You know," said Boggs as he glanced from Rob to Jared, "your friend Hills, he's got a real interesting family."

Jared gripped the kitchen counter edge so tight his knuckles turned white. He looked at Leisel, hoping to distract her, to give her a signal to leave, but she seemed absorbed in what Boggs was about to say.

"His daddy and mine are real tight, and I gotta admit that even though his old man's got some old-fashioned ideas, me and him think alike about some important stuff. Ain't that right, Jared?"

Boggs grinned and Jared felt Leisel and Rob looking at him too. "Shut up, Sam," he said.

Boggs ignored him and continued to talk to Leisel and Rob. "His dad runs a print shop. You guys have even seen some of his work, though I expect you didn't appreciate it the same way I do."

"I don't know what you're talking about," said Leisel. "You're just trying to make trouble."

"Right on," laughed Boggs. "But I'm also trying to get the truth out in the open. Let me make it short and sweet for you, babe. Jared's dad, he's the man that prints my favorite reading material. You know that anti-Momo stuff around town? Straight out of his dad's shop. And there's plenty more to come."

"What are you talking about?" asked Rob. "You mean that garbage in parking lots and stuff? Those pamphlets and flyers?"

"You got it." Boggs slapped him on the back. "Your buddy here, that's his family's main thing."

"Bull!" Rob pushed away from Boggs. "You're a liar."

Jared felt the heat rising up his neck. He wanted to throttle Boggs, to take him away from his friends and pound him.

"I don't get it." Leisel looked at Jared. "Your dad prints that stuff?"

"Right on, girl! Prints *and* distributes it." Boggs motioned his friends out the door. "You got it now so I guess we'll just head on out and find us a *real* party somewhere. See you 'round, Jared. Hope you have a really nifty new year." Boggs and his friends left laughing.

"What a jerk," Rob looked at Jared. "Saying stuff like that about your dad. He must already be high or something."

Jared studied the lines on the floor tile. Why now? Why did this have to happen now, tonight? Leisel would have found out soon enough, if she hadn't already guessed. And if she hadn't, he would have told her if for no other reason than her own safety. And Rob, well, he figured it'd be easier telling Rob. But he hadn't figured it would happen like this.

"As much as I hate Boggs," Jared sighed, "he's telling the truth." He couldn't stand the looks on their faces, but he kept on, letting the ugly truth spill into the room. "My dad's crazy or something. I don't know why or how he got that way. I hate what he does, guys. I even tried to talk him out of it once. I know I should have told you before, but—"

"Should have told us?" said Rob. "You should have stopped him. Should have called the cops. Geez, Jared, have you seen that junk he prints about our church?"

"Go easy, Rob," said Leisel. "It's not Jared's fault. Believe me, he's nothing like his dad."

"I know that, but I've read some of that stuff and it makes me sick. I've even had a run-in with a couple of their dudes when they were putting that stuff around on cars. A few years ago, I came out of Safeway and saw these two men covering windshields with anti-Mormon junk, so I start ripping it off. Pretty soon this guy comes over and hassles me. Then his buddy joins him. Two grown men and I was just a junior high kid. They shoved me around a little, cussed and swore and told me to get out of there before I got hurt."

Jared paled. "That was you?"

"What, did your old man and his Nazi buddies brag about it? Bet they had a lot of laughs about how they scared off the little Mormon kid."

"Even if they did," said Leisel, "you can't blame Jared for his dad."

"Yeah, but he could have told us." Rob shook his head. "I mean, Jared, we're buds and all that, but I had no clue your old man had a couple screws loose."

"Look," said Jared, growing desperate, "you guys know me . . ."

"Of course we do, and we like you even if your dad is a Nazi." Rob smiled but Jared didn't notice.

"I'm sorry, you guys. Really." Jared's voice cracked. "I am not like my dad. I hate what he does and I have nothing to do with it."

"All right, we know you're not the bad guy, but as a friend, you should've said something a long time ago."

"If your dad was some kind of ultra-weirdo, would you spread it around school?"

"I wouldn't let my dad hurt my friends."

"It's different with you," said Leisel. "Your dad wouldn't do anything like that. It's not fair for you to say what you'd do in Jared's situation because you're not in it; you'll never be in anything even close to it."

"I know, I know," said Rob, "but you gotta admit, it *is* a major surprise."

Jared hadn't moved. The ugliness that had been bared made him feel dirty and humiliated in front of his best friends. He had to get out of there, away from them, fast, so he left the kitchen and went out the front door.

Minutes later, Leisel found him sitting on a low brick fence in a corner of the front yard.

"Are you OK?" She stood in front of Jared, the streetlight casting her shadow over him.

"Leisel," he spoke without looking up, "I'm sorry. About Boggs, about my dad and what he does, about Rob. It's all true, and Rob's right: I should have done something, said something a long time ago." Tears rimmed his eyes and he was afraid to look at her, afraid that she wouldn't listen, wouldn't stay with him.

"Look," he said, "I'll understand if you want to go home now. I'll see if I can find you a ride." Jared moved to stand up, but she stopped him.

She smiled, that gorgeous smile, the same smile that he had permanently preserved in the crystal frame on his desk at home.

"Don't be stupid. It's not even midnight yet." Then she hugged him and whispered, "You're not your dad. Believe me, I know." She held him tighter. "What you need, Mr. Hills, is a walk, a romantic midnight stroll." She tugged him to his feet. "Come on, walk with me."

Holding hands, they walked down the street, and Jared felt a connection, a security he'd never experienced before. When they got to the corner, Leisel leaned against Jared, looked up into the night sky, and exhaled. "You know what I always think about on New Year's? I like to get outside like this where I can be alone and see the sky. Then I try to guess where I'll be and what I'll be doing one year from now."

"Leisel," said Jared, "about my dad and that stuff he does, I really do hate it. Believe me, if there was anything I could—"

She put her finger against his lips. "I'm not worried about your dad and what he does. I'm not even worried about you. I know you, Jared, and I know how good you are. That's why," she let her arm drop to her side, "that's why I love you." She leaned into him and he wrapped his arms around her. They stood there for a long time without talking, without moving.

Together.

On their way back to the party, Jared stopped and looked up at the stars. "You know," he said as he squeezed Leisel's hand, "next year at this same time, I want to be with you." Then he kissed her in the shadows in front of Becker's house, and as they kissed, clocks all over town chimed midnight, igniting the snaps, crackles, and explosions that ring in the new year.

"Wow!" said Leisel after their kiss. "When you kiss me, I hear fireworks."

"Planned it that way," Jared grinned and led her back into the party.

———————

They spent the rest of the party sitting in the kitchen together. Jared had never felt so happy, so at peace. *This new year,* he thought as he gazed at Leisel, *is going to be the best ever.*

Rob showed up at 12:40, keys dangling from one hand. "Look, Leisel, I'll drive you guys over to your house so you'll be home on time and then you or your dad can drop Jared at his place whenever." After the scene with Boggs, Jared felt uncomfortable and guilty around Rob and couldn't bring himself to look him in the face. Rob didn't seem to notice. "Then I'm going to come back and see this party, my very last high school New Year's Eve party, to the early morning end. You guys ready?"

———————

Rather than take the freeway home and, as Rob said, "battle the drunks and the crazies," Rob planned to take one of the quiet back roads that led from Becker's house east of Mesa back into town.

"Long as we're home by 1:00," said Leisel as they walked out to Rob's

CHRIS CROWE

car. She got in front and Jared closed her door and got in back. He instinc-
tively reached for his seat belt but remembered it was broken. No matter.
They'd be home soon anyway.

"Rob," Jared asked, "you OK to drive?"

"No problem," said Rob. "I'll get us there in plenty of time."

"No. Are you OK to drive? You had anything to drink?" Jared knew the
answer as soon as the doors were closed. He could smell the sickly sweet
scent of alcohol.

"Couple beers, but hey, you can trust me, old friend." Rob put his
hand on the ignition to start the car. "You want me to get out and walk a
straight line for you, Officer Hills?"

Leisel looked from Rob to Jared to her watch. "No," she said, "just be
careful. And get me home on time."

Becker's house was in a subdivision that had once been cotton fields
several miles east of town. Once out of the subdivision, Rob turned west
on an old farm road that led through the darkness to the distant glow of
downtown Mesa.

It was warm with the three of them in the car, so Rob rolled down his
window and sped up. Jared knew that the fresh air would help Rob clear
his head, so he rolled down his window too.

They hadn't gone more than a few miles when the road turned to
gravel.

"You sure you know where you're going?" asked Jared.

"Cool it, man," said Rob. "I'll get us there."

"I hope we're not late," said Leisel. "I don't want to spend the rest of
my vacation grounded."

As their car bounced down the road, Rob started looking confused.
"I'm pretty sure I know where we're going," he muttered. "There ought to
be a turn up here pretty soon."

Sure enough, the headlights revealed a fork in the road ahead. "Hey,
Jared, right or left?"

100

"Left," said Jared. "It'll take us back to a real road."

Rob looked unsure, then swerved to the road on the right. "No, this is the one. I'm sure now." The little car fishtailed into the turn and Rob accelerated onto the new road.

"You know," said Jared, "if we got lost out here in these fields, we're going to be big-time late and Leisel's dad will kill me *and* you."

"Relax," Rob said. "We'll be there before you know it." The Honda sped down the gravel road, its headlights cutting through the dusty darkness ahead.

Without warning, the road veered sharply to the left and Rob missed the turn. Too late to turn, barely enough time to slam on the brakes and hold on. The wheels screamed and skidded across the gravel and kicked up a huge dust cloud, but the car didn't stop.

Leisel screamed and threw her arms in front of her face; Rob swore, and Jared watched in horror as their car sped toward the concrete irrigation gate.

The car slammed into it, crunching metal and shattering cement. Its front end snagged on the edge of the gate, sending the car into a slow flip. On impact, the windshield shattered, spraying glass throughout the car. The force of the collision wrenched Jared's door open and sent him flying into the field, clipping his shoulder on the door as he was thrown free. He landed on his back, hard, struggled for breath, then blacked out.

When he came to, he wasn't sure where he was or what had happened. His right shoulder throbbed and his mouth tasted like copper. But in seconds his head cleared and he remembered everything. He tried to push himself to his feet to search for Leisel and Rob, but his arm buckled and he tumbled back into the dirt. Slowly, more carefully, he worked his feet under himself, stood up, and waited for the dizziness to subside. He held his breath and looked around; the field was quiet as a graveyard. About ten yards to his left, he saw Rob's wrecked Honda, a dark silhouette upside down in the field. One headlight still hanging in its grille cast a dim beam of light onto the ground. Jared stumbled toward the car, yelling for Leisel.

He found Rob inside the wreckage, still strapped in his seat. Rob groaned when Jared reached through the gaping hole where the window used to be and shook him. "Rob, hey, Rob!" Jared shook him again. "Where is she?" Battling the panic that burned inside him, he released Rob's seat belt and pulled him through the window. Rob was groggy, barely conscious.

"Where is she?" Jared cried. "What happened to her?"

Rob wobbled against Jared. "I, uh . . . , I don't know." His speech was slurred, slow. "It happened too fast. Oh, man, I can't even believe this . . ."

When Jared's eyes adjusted to the darkness, he let go of Rob and scanned the ground around the overturned car. "Come on, we've got to find her!" Desperation forced him to ignore the pounding ache in his head and shoulders until he found her, saved her. Squinting to see in the dusty darkness, he moved farther away from the wreck, and his stomach lurched when he saw one of her shoes on the ground. He continued his frantic search until, in shadows ahead of the car, he saw her.

"There she is!" he yelled. "Leisel! Leisel!" Jared stumbled to her and with trembling hands dragged her into the dim light from the car. "Come on, come on," he pleaded as he pulled her into his lap. "Come on, Leisel." Her hair was damp and sticky, her body limp, and Jared rocked her back and forth to get her to open her eyes, to show some sign of life. She didn't respond, and the reality of what had happened triggered a whirlwind in his head and set his heart pounding so hard that he could barely breathe.

"Run!" he screamed at Rob. "Get help! Go get some help!" Rob staggered backward, then turned and stumbled down the road.

The scene turned quiet and cold. Leisel didn't move or make a sound. Jared cradled her in his lap, her blonde hair spilling over his legs, and whispered, "Please, God, don't let her die. Oh, please, not now, not here."

But even as he pled, and cried, and mourned, he knew it was too late. Too late. The hurt and despair and awful ache mushroomed inside him until he thought he would explode.

Or die.

chapter 10

They weren't supposed to talk about their mission release dates, but Jared forgave his new companion for asking. "Three more weeks," he said. "I'll be home by the middle of January."

They sat on a low wooden bench on the edge of a small playground, waiting a few minutes before going to their next appointment. Despite the cold, it was still dry, and a few children bundled up in winter coats played on the swings and slides under the watchful eyes of their mothers.

"You'll probably stay in Himeji," said Jared, "and get a new senior companion." He leaned back on the bench, squinted into the sun, and sighed. "Man, I'm going to miss Japan."

"I'm going to miss it too," said Elder Newcomb. "When I leave, I mean. Boy, that first day, I didn't think I'd ever get used to missionary life here, but you know, it's not so bad. It's different, *totally* different, but different's not bad, is it?"

Jared nodded. In the sandbox in the center of the park, a pair of two-year-olds were fighting a turf-and-toy battle. One would take the other's toy and scurry over to his side of the sandbox. Then the other retaliated by running over to take a different toy back to his side. They sallied back and forth until finally the battle climaxed with one dumping a bucket of sand on the head of the other. At that point, both mothers ran over, apologizing to each other and scolding their children.

"That kid sure knows how to get even," Newcomb laughed. "I bet that other kid's mother will spend all night getting the sand out of his hair."

The mothers separated the two, brushed off the sand, and within seconds, the kids were playing with each other again.

"Wouldn't it be nice," said Jared, "if all our conflicts could be resolved that easily? Get mad, heave a bucket of sand, then have Mom come in and end it for you so you could go on enjoying your friend's company."

"Yeah," said Newcomb, "but when we get older, our memories get better and we hold grudges. I remember when I was in third grade, this kid, Paul O'Brien, used to take my milk money every day. Every single day on the way to school, he'd wait for me, take my money, and shove me to the ground. I'd cry all the rest of the way to school. I kept wanting to get even, but Mom told me to 'turn the other cheek,' and she quit sending money to school with me. I thought, 'OK, I can turn the other cheek, but I'll never forgive him for as long as I live.'"

"What happened?" asked Jared.

"When he realized I no longer had any money with me, he started ripping off Johnny Palmer, the kid I walked to school with. Only," Elder Newcomb smiled, "he didn't know that Johnny had three older brothers. I think he got Johnny's money once or twice before Johnny's brothers pounded him and made him pay us *both* back all the money he'd taken, plus interest."

Elder Newcomb's smile widened. "I was able to forgive him after that."

They both laughed. Jared felt a kinship with this odd but likeable elder, a feeling that surprised him. A week ago he thought he'd never be able to accept—much less love—a companion like Newcomb, but it had happened, and Jared was glad. Maybe he was finally maturing, finally learning true charity.

"You know," said Newcomb, "you never finished telling me about your old friend Bob. What happened after that wreck? I bet you wanted to kill him."

"I guess that was my very first reaction, but it wouldn't have done any of us any good." Jared took a deep breath. "No, when I finally got over my anger, I mainly felt sorry for Rob."

*   *   *   *   *

Jared's father handled the news of the accident surprisingly well.

"What do you expect when you hang around with idiots?" he had asked Jared in the emergency room at the hospital. His parents stood next to the gurney where he lay in a medicated haze.

"You know, you're lucky you're not—" He stopped when Jared's mother touched his shoulder. Jared's father glared at her before continuing. "I mean, I'm glad you're not hurt too bad. But you can't say I didn't warn you." He looked at Jared, then at his wife, and turned to leave. "I gotta find someplace where they'll let me smoke."

Jared's mother watched him go, then gently stroked Jared's forehead just as she had when he was younger and had a fever. When she finally spoke, her voice trembled. "I'm terribly sorry to hear about your friend. I've been sitting with her mother," she nodded toward the waiting room, "offering whatever comfort I could. Oh, Jared, it's so sad; so, so awful . . ." She broke into tears.

"But Leisel's not . . ." Jared couldn't say the word. Didn't want to believe it. Could not believe it. Just a few hours earlier, they'd been together, happy. Maybe even in love. No, he was sure she was OK. He *knew* she was OK. The wreck had all been a bad dream. Had to be. He willed it to be. But in the pit of his stomach, a hollow ache gnawed at him. Everything seemed cloudy, foggy.

"Mom?" His own voice seemed far away. "Mom, she's OK, isn't she? I mean, she'll *be* OK, right?"

His mother's face showed only sadness and pain. "The injuries were too severe, son. It was too late to save her. They tried, I know they tried . . ." She covered her mouth and sobbed. "Oh, Jared, I'm so sorry."

The pain and medication were making it difficult for him to think clearly. His mother was crying. Said they tried to save her. Who? Leisel? He concentrated, hard. Injuries too severe? Then an image flashed in his memory: the shadow of Rob's car in the field, Leisel limp in his arms, darkness all around.

"No." He cried softly at first, then more loudly. "No, no, no!" He pounded on the gurney until his arms grew limp and the pain and drugs and bottomless sadness overwhelmed him. He faded fast then, and the last thing he remembered was his mother watching helplessly as sleep and despair engulfed him.

———————

Jared traveled home from the hospital in the twilight zone between sleep and consciousness, but he distinctly heard one thing his father said:

"Your mother and I talked about this religion stuff while we were waiting at the hospital."

"This can wait till he's feeling better," said Jared's mother.

"No. I want to get it out and over with. Jared, if you want to mix with Mormons, it's up to you, but you gotta be willing to accept the consequences. It's something you're going to have to live with for the rest of your life. It won't be pleasant, and I'm not going to be responsible for any of it."

Jared felt no joy at finally being given backhanded permission to continue to investigate the Church. With Leisel gone, he wasn't sure anything mattered anymore.

When they got home, he trudged up the stairs and collapsed into bed.

From there he could see Leisel's photo on his desk. He loved her, but thinking of her and the love he had for her and realizing that she was gone, dead—well, that love now meant nothing. Nothing but pain and sadness. He reached over and picked up the crystal-framed photo. He took a long look at Leisel, her bright smiling face, then put the photo face down in his desk drawer and closed it.

———————

Leisel's father called the next day. "Just wanted to see if you're OK," he said, his voice flat and hollow.

Jared didn't know how to respond.

"The doctor," he continued, "said you broke your collarbone and took a hard shot on your head, but other than that, you're in pretty good shape."

"Yeah," said Jared. What do you say to a man whose daughter has just been killed?

"Good, I'm glad. You know, her funeral . . . ," his voice cracked and he paused a moment. "I'm sorry. This is hard." He paused again before continuing. "Leisel's funeral is going to be on the fifth. If you're up to it, we'd like you to . . . she would have liked you to be there. And to say a few words."

Jared was crying now. He thought he had cried all the emotion out of himself, but hearing the pain in Leisel's father's voice was more than he could bear.

"I'm sorry," Jared sobbed. "I'm so, so sorry for everything. I shouldn't have let Rob drive. We should have gone another way. Oh, man." He took a deep breath to steady his voice, but it still shuddered when he said, "I miss her so bad."

"We all do, son," the warmth had returned to her father's voice. "That's why we want you with us at her funeral. Will you come?"

"I don't know if I could stand it. To see her brothers and Michelle and you and her mom. To think about her lying there . . ."

"We'd help you. We're all sad, Jared. We all miss her, but we want you with us at the funeral. The boys—Enoch especially—need you to be there. Every one of us is hurting right now, and we'll be hurting for a long time, but this will help us to get over it."

His words soothed Jared. "OK. I'll come. I'll be there."

"She would have wanted you there. I think you know that. And, Jared?"

"Yeah?"

"I want you to know that what happened does not change how we feel about you. The accident wasn't your fault. The boys, Michelle, my wife and I, we all still feel like you're a part of our family. None of us want that to change."

"Thanks. Thanks for saying that." As he hung up the phone, Jared still felt sad, but the feeling of utter despair that had dogged him since the accident lifted.

———————

The stake center overflowed with family, kids from school, and people from Church. Jared, his arm in a sling, sat with Leisel's parents on the stand. It was the first time he had ever been to a funeral, and it was only his second LDS meeting.

As bishop of Leisel's ward, Rob's father conducted the service. He spoke warmly of Leisel, of her good qualities and character, but his words couldn't mask the pain in his voice. Jared sat numb on the stand listening to Bishop Whitman, barely hearing him as he stared through a blur of tears at the shiny grey casket that held Leisel. He knew that he had to speak next. He had thought about what he wanted to say, but he didn't know if he'd be able to say anything. He still hurt that bad.

When the bishop sat down, Leisel's father smiled and said, "Speak from your heart, son," and patted Jared on the back.

Jared stood and looked over the congregation, many of them friends from school, then looked down at the casket in front of the stand. "I . . . I don't know what to say, exactly. A lot of you knew her a lot longer than I did, and some of you may have even known her better than I did. Leisel was a good, a great girl; she was my friend." He took a breath to steady his voice. "And like all of you, I'm going to miss her." Several people in the congregation were crying openly. Jared ignored his own tears as he continued.

"Sometimes in life, we meet special people, really special people who make our lives better just for having known them. Leisel was that kind of a person. I've never ever known anyone like her." He paused and let out a shaky sigh. "And I'll be grateful forever that she was my friend." From behind him he heard her mother crying. "I loved her, love her, . . . and I hope Heavenly Father can bless me—and all of us—to get along without her." He paused to wipe the tears from his cheeks. "Good-bye, Leisel," he said and sat down so full of sadness that he thought he would explode.

Leisel's Laurel teacher spoke, then Leisel's parents, and they were sad, but not despairing. Jared marveled at their ability to face this awful tragedy. Unfortunately, their words offered him little comfort. Leisel was gone.

Gone forever.

After the funeral, Jared found out that Rob hadn't attended. At first he thought that injuries from the accident prevented him from coming, but he learned from Leisel's father that Rob had refused to come.

"I can't blame him," said Mr. Lee. "Still, I wish he had been there to hear what was said. I think it would have made him feel better. If you see him, Jared, will you talk to him for us? Tell him we have no hard feelings, and staying away from us, and especially from the Church, won't help him get over this."

When Jared got home, he called Rob.

"Yeah?"

"Just thought I'd call to see if you're OK and everything."

No response.

"Leisel's funeral was this afternoon."

"Look, I don't know what you want from me." Rob sounded shaky. "I know she's dead, and I feel worse about it than anybody. I had no right to be at her funeral."

"If you want to talk about it, I'll come over and—"

"I can barely face myself, how am I going to face you or anybody else who knew her? This is something I've got to work out alone. It's my problem—I'm the one, the one who killed her—and I've got to solve it by myself."

Rob hung up before Jared could respond. He tried calling back several times, but Rob never answered.

That evening, Jared went to the visitors' center at the Mesa Temple. He wasn't sure why he went there; maybe it was just the need to be where he and Leisel had been together. He walked through the center, not looking so much as remembering. Remembering being with Leisel.

"Excuse me." It was one of the visitors' center's missionaries. "Do you have any questions about our exhibits?" His eyes lit up. "Say, aren't you the young man who came here several times with that attractive young woman?"

Jared nodded.

"I took a photograph of you two out front, remember? A handsome couple." Before he could say more, a worker from the front desk called him to lead a tour. "Well," he said, "looks like I'm needed. But you know your way around here already."

Jared left the center and wandered the grounds for a few minutes, finally stopping to sit on the edge of the reflection pond, where he could look up at the temple.

"Oh, Leisel," he whispered. "What am I going to do?" Memories of her flooded his thoughts. He remembered her excitement when he agreed to take the missionary discussions, and later when he committed to be baptized. It seemed like a million years ago. With her gone, did any of it matter now? Would anyone care? Would being a member of the Church make any real difference in his life?

He realized he was at a crossroads and he knew that the road he chose would change his life forever.

chapter 11

Elder Newcomb sat mesmerized by Jared's story. Finally, he spoke. "Oh, man, that's a beautiful story." He reached under his glasses with one finger and wiped away a tear. "It's just like they taught us in the MTC. When you find someone who's ready and challenge them to really pray about baptism, the Spirit will convert them. You know, I had this one MTC instructor who always harped on that. 'Missionaries don't convert people, the Spirit does. Your job, Elders, is to prepare people to feel the promptings of the Holy Ghost.'

"But, you know, I was born in the Church, so I wasn't really sure how it worked. But it worked for you, didn't it? Oh man, what a beautiful story. That's what I want to do. I want to find people here in Japan who are prepared like you were, and I want to teach them the gospel so the Spirit can convert them." Newcomb paused. "Only problem is, I'm scared to death. Streeting the other day, that was fun and everything, but honestly, Elder Hills, I don't think I can be any good in a real missionary discussion. My Japanese is terrible, and I'm afraid I'll talk too much or offend someone, or do something stupid and ruin someone's chance to accept the gospel."

"Don't worry about it." Jared patted Newcomb on the back. "All missionaries feel that way at first. It is scary, mainly because it's such an awesome responsibility. But you can do it. The Lord will help you. And so will I."

Newcomb brightened. "You really think I can do it? Honestly?"

"Positive."

"Well, I promise I'm going to give it my very best effort. No more locking myself in the bathroom. It's time to roll up my sleeves and get into the work." Newcomb grinned. "I'm doing the right thing, I know it," his smile faded, "but missionary work still scares me a little."

"Me too," said Jared.

"Really? I mean, you've been out here a long time and I just figured, well, I thought that it was routine for you."

"In some ways, I guess it is, but it's still intimidating."

"Were you like me when you first got here?" Newcomb saw the look on Jared's face and laughed. "I don't mean *exactly* like me, but did you ever wonder if maybe you had made a big mistake?"

"I guess I did a few times. You know, right after I got baptized, I thought I was done making all those hard spiritual decisions, that everything would be easy from then on out. But that was only the beginning. I had never even dreamed of going on a mission."

Newcomb threw a clumsy arm over Jared's shoulder. "Well, I've got to tell you, Elder, I'm awfully glad you did."

Jared smiled. "So am I, Elder. So am I."

*   *   *   *   *

Leisel's father baptized Jared two weeks after the funeral. It was a small service. Rob didn't come, but the missionaries, Bishop Whitman, Jared's mother, and the Lee family were there. For Jared, it was a somber occasion. He felt a spirit of comfort, but he also felt an empty longing for Leisel, a longing he knew her family shared.

After Bishop Whitman confirmed Jared, Enoch broke into the circle to shake his hand. "Congratulations, *Brother* Hills," he said with a crooked smile. Jared took his hand and pulled Enoch into his lap where he hugged him and tried not to cry.

The men in the circle added their congratulations. Still holding Enoch, Jared stood up to receive hugs from Sister Lee and the Lee kids, and from his mother.

"Hey, Jared," asked Enoch, "you still going to come over on Sundays and eat with us?"

Jared hesitated. He knew it would be too painful for him to visit Leisel's house so soon. "Maybe I will, a little later."

Sister Lee smiled and patted Enoch on the head. "Well, consider it an open invitation, Jared. You know we'd love to have you come over any time."

Being a member of the Church and having the priesthood didn't change Jared as much as he thought it would. He felt an inner peace, but life wasn't any easier. He would have had to work hard to avoid religious arguments with his dad had they been speaking at all. The only regular communication Jared received from his father was an occasional anti-Mormon pamphlet left on his desk.

His new membership in the Church and his growing understanding of the gospel did little to help him cope with Leisel's death. He still felt miserable without her. And a week after the accident, he started having nightmares. Sometimes he'd wake up in the middle of the night thinking that it had all been a dream. He'd lie awake believing Leisel was still alive, but too soon, reality would intrude to remind him that she was dead.

And that he was alone.

He didn't regret his decision to join the Church, but without Rob and Leisel, Church and school weren't the same anymore. After the accident, Rob refused to attend Church, refused for a long time even to talk to

Jared about it. And when the coach suspended him from the team for breaking training rules, Rob, already depressed because of the accident, dropped out of school. "I need to get my head together," he explained to Jared. "And I don't think I can do that around here."

"But you've got less than a semester left before you graduate."

"I didn't say I wouldn't come back and finish. Maybe summer school or something, but school and all the rest of this stuff," he sighed, "is not what I need right now."

"What's your dad think?"

"It really doesn't matter what he thinks. Heck, I'm lucky I'm not in *jail*. If the Lees would have pressed charges . . ."

"They're not like that."

"Yeah, but if they had. No, I need time away, time to think things out."

"What about Church?"

Rob smirked. "That's the last place I want to be. I was a lousy member before all this. What are they going to think of me now? Besides, I'm not even sure if I buy into all that."

"But doesn't it make more sense to try to work it out inside the Church instead of outside? People there care about you; they'd help you out. I know it."

"You're wasting your time, man. I can't go back there until I get things settled."

"How long?" Jared asked.

"Long as it takes." He looked at Jared sadly. "Maybe a real long time."

Jared saw little of Rob after that, but from what he did see and hear about Rob, he knew that instead of pulling things back together, Rob was drifting farther and farther away.

"It's really hard," Jared told Bishop Whitman in an interview several months after his baptism, "to stop thinking about Leisel." He struggled to control the sadness in his voice. "I've started having these nightmares about the accident—they're so real—and I keep missing the chance to save her. They end the same way every time and I wake up scared and depressed all over again.

"And I can't even talk about it to Rob," he continued. "I don't blame him for the wreck, but he doesn't believe me. I wish I could talk to him about it. Maybe, somehow, it would help. But I hardly ever even see him anymore."

"He's really mixed up right now," said the bishop. "Even though I wish there was something you could do to help him, I really don't think he's ready. At least not the way he's feeling now. But don't give up on him, Jared, even if he makes you feel like you'd want to."

"It's just," Jared looked down into his lap, "it's so hard to handle this alone. Mom tries, and she does help some, but, oh man, Bishop, I wish I had a good friend to talk to."

"You're still hurting, aren't you?"

"Yeah," said Jared. "It really hurts to lose one friend, but then to lose the other too. . . . I thought getting baptized would help. But sometimes," he looked up at the bishop, "sometimes I wonder if I did the right thing. I mean, shouldn't I be happy? And if I should, why am I still feeling so terrible?"

The bishop leaned forward in his chair. "What you're feeling is normal, Jared. Joining the Church doesn't make you any less human. Going through what you have in the last month would be hard for anyone. It's been hard for me too, you know."

Jared nodded. He hadn't thought about the burden of grief Bishop Whitman must be carrying.

"But we know that life won't be easy. People live and die. Tragedies happen. People disappoint us. That's all part of living on this earth. And we learn and grow from the good and bad we experience. We can't always understand why things happen, and we can't always control what happens

117

to us, but we can make sure that we are living and doing right so that no matter what happens, we keep it in an eternal perspective."

"So what does that mean for me?"

"That means that you keep on doing what you have been doing. Study the gospel, keep the commandments, and serve the Lord. There are no guarantees that you'll have a perfectly happy life. As a matter of fact, you most likely still have plenty of trials left to face. But if you're doing all you can, at the end of your life you can be content, and that's what true happiness is. It's not an absence of suffering and unhappiness, it's a confidence that you're doing the Lord's will."

"But it's not easy."

"No, it's not easy, but when you do what's right, Jared, you're blessed, sometimes in ways you can't even recognize."

He and the bishop talked for a few more minutes before Jared stood up to leave.

"One more thing," said the bishop. "Have you ever thought about a mission?"

Jared shook his head. "Between my dad's attitude and my lack of money, I figured it was something I wouldn't be able to do."

"The Lord wants you to serve, Jared. And because he wants you to, the way will be opened for you to go. You just have to be willing." He looked Jared in the eye with a gaze that penetrated to his soul. "Are you?"

"I don't know," said Jared. "I'm going to have to think about it."

Jared drove home that evening, confused and unsettled about a mission. *What right did the bishop have to put me on the spot like that? He knows what I've been through, he knows my dad is a radical anti-Mormon, he knows I don't have the money for a mission.* Despite his rationalizing, he couldn't shake the feeling he had had when the bishop told him the Lord wanted him to serve. He needed to talk to someone, to work out his feelings, to find out what he should do.

The front porch light cast an amber glow onto the driveway of Leisel's house, and Jared pulled his car to the edge of the circle of light and looked at his watch. 9:30. The boys would be in bed by now, but Leisel's dad would still be up.

"Jared?" Leisel's mother answered the door. "Is everything OK?"

"I just wondered if I could talk to Brother Lee about a couple things. He's not in bed yet, is he?"

"Go sit in the kitchen and I'll run downstairs and tell him you're here." She nodded toward the kitchen door. "And there's a bunch of cookies in the cookie jar. Help yourself."

He sat at the kitchen table and munched on a peanut butter chocolate chip cookie and wondered if he had done the right thing to come here. But he didn't know who else to turn to, who else to ask for advice. Besides, it felt good to be in Leisel's house again.

The kitchen door opened and Brother Lee walked in. "Jared, it's great to have you over here again. Danny and Enoch have been asking when you'd come visit us. They'll be upset you didn't come a little earlier." He sat in the chair across from Jared. "So, to save my own reputation around here, promise me something."

"Yeah?"

"Dinner. Next Sunday. If you don't, the boys will have my hide."

Jared agreed to come.

"Thanks. Now I might be able to get some respect around here again. The boys have been blaming me for your recent absence. So, what's up?"

Jared told him about his interview with Bishop Whitman, especially the part about the mission.

"And you're not sure you want to go?"

"It's not that I think missions are a bad idea; I know what the prophet has said about missions and everything, but I just never thought that applied to me. You know, I'm still a brand-new member. And my parents would hate the idea of me being a Mormon missionary." He ran his hand through his hair. "I don't know what to do. It's hard to imagine telling the bishop no, but it's even harder to imagine me on a mission." Jared stopped, waiting for Brother Lee to respond.

Instead of speaking, Leisel's father sat quietly, his eyes fixed on Jared.

"Well," asked Jared, "what do you think I should do?"

"You know," Brother Lee smiled as he spoke, "I can remember when I started thinking seriously about a mission. It scared me to death, and I'd been a member all my life."

"So what'd you do?"

"Talked to my dad. I asked him what you just asked me, to tell me what to do."

"And what did he tell you?"

"Same thing I'm going to tell you: It's not my call, son. I can't tell another man what he should or shouldn't do. If you really want to know, you'll have to pray about it. The Lord'll let you know what you should do."

"But what if He tells me to go?"

"Then you go. It'll work out. You'll be blessed."

That definitely wasn't the advice he expected, and at first, Brother Lee's non-answer made Jared angry. The last thing Jared wanted was to wrestle with yet another major decision. But as he left the Lee's house that night, he knew that the Lord would answer his prayer about serving a mission. And even as got into his car to drive home, he knew what the Lord's answer would be.

And he knew what his own answer would be too.

chapter 12

Two weeks had passed. Elder Newcomb's Japanese was rapidly improving because of the time he spent talking to children at the local playgrounds. Speaking Japanese to kids was somehow less inhibiting and gave him the practice he so badly needed.

Jared had less than a week left on his mission, and as he watched his companion kicking a soccer ball around with a group of Japanese children, he felt a twinge of homesickness, not for Arizona, but for Japan. He'd miss the country and its people; he'd miss being a missionary. And he was surprised to realize that he'd miss his companion. Elder Newcomb had learned to overcome his fears—he was still goofy, but Jared liked him anyway. He had turned into a solid companion.

Jared watched Newcomb chatting and laughing with the boys he had been playing with, noticing that one boy in particular seemed intent on carrying on a conversation with him. After a few exchanges, Newcomb's eyebrows shot up in surprise. The boy smiled and nodded to a question Newcomb asked. Newcomb pointed at Jared and as the boy looked, the elder continued to talk to him. Their conversation ended with them bowing to one another and shaking hands.

Grinning like a kindergartner on his way to recess, Newcomb lumbered over to the bench where Jared sat.

"Make a new friend?" Jared asked.

"Oh, man, you won't believe it." Newcomb's cheeks were red from the cold. "That kid, Masuhiro, when I told him we were missionaries, he started asking a bunch of questions. So I told him we were from America and that we were here to talk to people about Jesus Christ."

"And that's when the conversation ended, right?"

"Wrong." Newcomb sat down next to Jared. "That's when he started asking a bunch more questions. He wanted to know if we were Mormons, and I thought, 'Wow, this is only my third week and already I've found a golden contact.' Anyway, I told him yes, we were.

"You know, my mom always said something like this would happen. If I'd just be myself, she said, and have faith, good things would happen on my mission; the Lord would direct the right people to me. It never occurred to me that it might *really* happen, not that I thought it couldn't happen, but, you know . . ."

Jared nudged him. "Get on with the story about the kid. What did he want to know?"

"Oh, yeah, sorry. Well, Masuhiro told me that his parents had wanted to talk to some Mormon missionaries once, but they missed the appointment when their grandfather got sick and everybody went to the hospital with him. His father has been out of town and busy at work, so they just sort of gave up on the idea. Anyway, I asked him if they might still be interested and he said yes, and I asked if he thought it would be OK if we dropped by his house tonight after dinner and he said sure. So we got an appointment. My first appointment!"

"So who are these guys?"

"That's the good part. Remember that family that stood us up my first night?"

"The Terauchis?"

Newcomb nodded. "That kid was Masuhiro Terauchi. They're still interested. Oh, man, I have a really good feeling about this. I know they're going to listen to us."

Jared smiled. This wasn't the first time he'd been led to golden investigators, but it was one of the few. He had a good feeling about them too. "Good job, Elder." He slapped Newcomb on the back. "That was a super piece of missionary work. If things go right, we might get that whole family on track to be baptized before I leave."

Newcomb beamed. "It wasn't really that hard. When he asked me where I was from, it seemed natural to start talking about the Church. Heck, it wasn't hard at all. And you know what? I didn't even realize I was speaking Japanese. It just flowed out."

Jared grinned. "I think you're going to make it."

"Huh?"

"I think you're going to make an awesome missionary, Elder."

"Well, Elder Hills," asked President Mizuno at the conclusion of his final interview, "are you ready to return home?"

"I guess so, but I'm not sure what it's going to be like back there. When I left, things were pretty complicated."

The president reassured him things would be fine and thanked him again for serving faithfully in the mission. "You've served well, Elder. I'm sure the Lord will bless you for serving in Japan." Then he shook his hand and walked with him to the door.

"You know, President, I'm going to miss Japan, and my companion. When I first met him, I thought, 'Oh wow, what a miserable way to end my mission. This weirdo's going to drive me crazy.' But eventually I learned to love the guy. He taught me a ton about charity and accepting people who are different from me." Jared paused and thought about his companion once more. "You know, Elder Newcomb turned out to be a pretty darn good missionary."

"That is why I assigned him to you as his first companion. I knew you would train him well."

Jared smiled at the compliment. He was glad he hadn't let the president—or his companion—down.

*   *   *   *   *

Jared hadn't seen or heard from Rob in more than six months. When Rob dropped out of school, Jared would sometimes see him around the neighborhood, but a few months ago, Rob had gotten a job where he worked on Sundays. Jared tried to keep track of him by calling once in a while, but Rob never answered. He kept calling anyway, and one day he caught him, and this time, Rob didn't hang up. But he didn't say anything either.

"Hey, you're a hard guy to get a hold of, you know that?" Jared tried to sound lighthearted.

Rob grunted. "Been busy, man."

"I was hoping I could see you before I leave for my mission—I'm going to the Japan Hiroshima Mission, maybe your dad told you. Anyway, I'm speaking this Sunday, and I was wondering if you could come."

No reply.

"I'd really like to be able to say good-bye, Rob. And maybe talk. It's been a long time."

"Yeah, well, things have been kind of weird for me lately. And real busy. I don't know if I can get off work . . ."

"Look, I don't know why you've been dodging me. If there's something I've done to make you mad, I'm really sorry."

"You don't have anything to apologize for, Jared. My life's my own fault. I'm smart enough to know that."

"Then you're also smart enough to know I'm your friend. I want to see you; I want to talk before I'm gone. It'll be two years before I'm back. So will you come?"

"We'll see."

For Jared, that was good enough.

———

The first missionary farewell Jared ever attended was his own. He had been in the ward a little over a year, and already the people there, not just the Lees, but all the ward, seemed like extended family. He'd miss them, he would miss home, but he looked forward to serving a mission even though he had no idea what to expect from missionary life in Japan. He hoped and prayed he'd be up to it.

It almost looked like a normal Sunday. The Lee kids sat in the fourth row where they always sat. The bishopric was on the stand. But so was Jared. And so were Brother and Sister Lee and Brother Speares, his elders quorum president. They were all going to speak, and he was going to speak last. Jared's hands felt cold and sweaty. He hoped his talk would go well; he hoped Rob would come.

Bishop Whitman introduced the speakers and then said a few words about Jared. Brother Speares had served a mission to Japan several years ago and gave Jared some sound advice about perseverance and working in tune with the Holy Ghost. Then Sister Lee spoke, mostly about Leisel and what a great member missionary she had been. Brother Lee told experiences from his own mission and concluded by talking about the importance of serving missions.

Finally it was Jared's turn.

When he stood to speak, he saw Rob slip into the back of the chapel. He looked like he had just gotten out of bed.

Jared thanked the people who had helped him prepare for his mission, especially the Lees. "Someday," he said, "I hope I can have a family just like theirs. They're a celestial family, and I'm going to miss them while

I'm gone." His heart ached when he thought of them, and for a moment he couldn't speak. Finally, he said, "I'm really grateful to be here today, grateful to be going on a mission. As some of you know, there have been quite a few obstacles in my road into the Church, but I'm confident," he paused and looked at Rob, but Rob didn't look up, "I *know* that I chose the right road. There's a poem by Robert Frost we studied last year that describes what's happened to me. It's called 'The Road Not Taken.' Let me read part of it."

Jared smoothed out a paper that he had copied the poem on. He read slowly and clearly.

> "I shall be telling this with a sigh
> Somewhere ages and ages hence:
> Two roads diverged in a wood, and I—
> I took the one less traveled by,
> And that has made all the difference.

"Brothers and sisters, I know that the decisions we make put us on the roads that determine what kind of lives we'll have. I was lucky enough to have some friends who steered me onto the right road and have helped keep me on it." Rob was watching him now. "We all have moments when we stand at a crossroads, and when that happens, we should pray about the direction we want our lives to take and then have the courage to choose the right road. I hope that I'll always be able to do that, on my mission and after." He then bore his testimony and sat down.

After the meeting, several members of the ward congratulated him and wished him good luck on his mission. Rob lingered in the back of the chapel, waiting.

In a few minutes, the last of the well-wishers had left, leaving Jared and Rob alone in the chapel. Rob's hair had grown long and shaggy and his athletic frame now seemed rounder and softer. When Rob stood to greet him, Jared noticed that the cocky spark in Rob's eyes had been replaced by a blank indifference.

"Glad you could come." Jared held out his hand and Rob accepted it.

"I had today off, so I figured I might as well show up." He looked Jared up and down and poked the lapel of his suit. "Looking good, man. Just like a missionary. You know, even before you converted, you seemed like the type: clean cut, didn't drink or swear. Heck, my dad should've raised you instead of me."

"Hey, you can still go on a mission."

Rob laughed. "Yeah, right. My past isn't quite lily white, remember? And even *I* know that you got to believe in the product you're selling."

"And you don't?"

Rob sat down. "You don't know me as well as you think. A lot of bad stuff has happened this past year. And not just the accident either. But that's what started it. I still feel so guilty. . . . If only I had been more careful, if I hadn't been so stupid." He shook his head. "I don't know. Anyway, after that, I started questioning my parents, the Church, whether any of it really matters. It's not just a matter of whether or not I believe but really whether or not I want to live that kind of life, whether it's worth it to lead that kind of life. You know, it's funny, but before the accident, I think I really did plan to stay active, go on a mission and all that." Rob looked defeated. "Didn't turn out that way, did it?"

"No," said Jared, "but it doesn't have to end that way either."

"Well, I guess I'll have to wait and see." He stood, put an arm around Jared's shoulder and walked with him to the chapel door. "Look, I've got to split before my old man drags me to Sunday School. But I just wanted to say good luck over there in Japan. I know you'll do great."

Jared wrapped Rob in a clumsy bear hug. "Thanks," he said. "And thanks for coming. I'm really glad I got to see you again."

Rob just nodded. "See you, Jared," he said before leaving the chapel.

Left alone in the chapel, Jared sat on the back bench and put his face in his hands. He had been encouraged by seeing Rob at church, but after talking to him, he wasn't sure what Rob's future held. He offered a prayer that sooner or later Rob would get on the right road.

Then in the quiet of the empty chapel Jared cried.

For Rob. For Leisel.

And for himself.

chapter 13

Jared wasn't sure exactly who would be at the Phoenix airport to meet him. In their last letter, Brother and Sister Lee promised they'd be there, but he hadn't heard from his mom since he had written her to say when he'd be getting home.

As he headed for the baggage claim, his hands felt cold and his stomach twisted into a knot. Having been a missionary for two years, two years in *Japan,* he wasn't sure he still knew how to act around American people. And he knew that people change, that he had changed, and he didn't know how that would affect his relationships with his parents, the Lees, and his friends. He wondered if his father would even let him live at home anymore. The answer, he knew, would come pretty soon.

He had just cleared security when a blond blur flashed into him and grabbed him around the waist. "Jared! Hey, Jared, welcome back!"

He dropped his carry-on bags and knelt down to look the boy in the face. "Danny?"

"Not Danny," the boy pouted. "I'm *Enoch.* Don't you remember me?"

"Sure, I remember you, but didn't you used to be a lot smaller?"

"I'm baptized now," Enoch said proudly, his chest swelling a little.

"Come on, everybody's waiting." He took Jared by the hand and led him to the people waiting for him at the baggage carousel.

Jared scanned the faces. Brother and Sister Lee and the boys were there. His mom, teary-eyed. A couple of guys from the ward who had already returned from their missions. A tall girl, attractive with long blonde hair. His heart skipped. Leisel? She saw him smiling and waved back; Michelle had grown, and she looked an awful lot like her older sister.

He didn't see his father or Rob. He wasn't surprised, but he couldn't help feeling disappointed. Jared saw his mother move in close and held out his arms to embrace her. "Welcome back, son," she said as she hugged him. "I'm so glad to see you; I've really missed you."

"It's great to be home, Mom." Jared hesitated, then asked. "How's Dad?"

"He couldn't come," she said. "I'm afraid he hasn't changed much in two years."

Jared felt angry, then disappointed. "Do I still have a place to stay?"

"That much we've settled. I want you to stay."

Danny and Enoch had his bags now and led the way to the exit, the welcoming party and Jared trailing behind.

Jared looked around and felt good.

Really good.

———

He awoke the next morning with a kink in his back. Two years of sleeping on *futons* made his old bed seem too soft for him. The clock radio on his desk showed 4:58 A.M., but he couldn't sleep; jet lag and the excitement of being home woke him early. At first, he felt disoriented, not exactly sure where he was, then it came to him: home, he was home again, in his own room, his own bed. The house was quiet, and in the early morning darkness, he could hear the quiet hum of their central heating blowing warm air through the house. The warm air felt good. He swung his feet to the floor and stretched.

He stood up, stretched again, then went to his desk and switched on the study lamp. Most of the desktop had been packed away when Jared left for his mission, but a worn pocket dictionary, his clock radio, and a jar of pencils remained. He opened the desk drawer and pulled out the crystal-framed picture of Leisel he had put away more than two years ago. The frame sparkled under the lamplight, and Jared looked at it longingly.

He recalled that afternoon at the visitors' center when they had stood with their arms around each other and posed for that photo. He remembered the day, it seemed like forever ago, Leisel had given him the framed photo for Christmas. Then he thought again of Leisel and all the days he shared with her. The accident, the funeral, those were a part of his memories too, but now, finally, they seemed to fade in the light of the brighter, happier recollections he had of being with her. She had changed his life and he would never forget that, but, he realized, he could at last forget the pain.

There was enough good to remember.

He closed the drawer and placed the photo back on his desk, switched off the lamp, and got back into bed. Then it occurred to him that this morning was one of the few times in three years that his sleep had been disrupted by something other than the nightmare. Maybe he was finally free from all that. He hoped so. He was ready to get on with life.

———————

Jared went downstairs a few hours later. "Morning, Mom."

"Oh, you're up." She turned from the stove and hugged him. "I wanted to let you sleep as long as you needed to this morning." She pointed to a pan containing a Mexican omelet. "I wasn't sure if your tastes had changed after being in Japan for so long, but I remembered that you use to love my omelets. Will this be OK for breakfast?"

Jared inhaled the rich scent of green chilies and cheese. "It'll be awesome," he said. "Anything but *mugi*."

He sat at the kitchen table savoring the familiar smells and surroundings. With each passing hour, he felt more and more comfortable being home again, but there was still one thing he wanted to take care of before Church on Sunday. "Hey, Mom," he asked as she set his plate in front of him, "do you mind if I use the car today?"

———————

Driving to Rob's house, Jared realized that little had changed in Mesa in the two years he had been gone. Of course, there were a few new homes here and a couple new stores there, but the streets and sights were pretty much the same as they had been before he left.

Jared parked the car on the street in front of the Whitman's house and sat there a few minutes trying to decide whether or not to go up and knock on the door. "I should have called first," he said aloud. "He probably won't even be at home. And for all I know, he may not even want to talk to me." Jared thought about his last conversation with Rob. "He might not even live here anymore. I really should have called."

After stewing a few moments longer, Jared decided action was better than inaction and got out of the car, walked up to the front door, and rang the doorbell.

"Jared!" Sister Whitman wrapped him up in a hug. "I didn't think I'd get to see you until tomorrow at Church. Oh, welcome home." She pulled him into the house. "Come in, come in. Rob will be thrilled to see you."

"He's here?"

She nodded. "We've had some ups and downs, but he is here. I'll go get him," she said, and left Jared waiting in the living room.

Jared sat on the edge of the couch. The last time he had seen Rob, he was sure Rob was headed for disaster. Rob had been on the edge, just like Leisel had said, and when Jared left for his mission, it had seemed like Rob was ready to fall off.

He half expected to see him with a tattoo, or long hair, or a beer belly, but whatever Rob looked like, Jared promised himself that he would show love and acceptance. He'd use what he learned on his mission, and he'd work hard to activate Rob.

"Yo, Jared!"

Jared looked up. No long hair, no tattoos, no beer belly. In fact, Rob looked bigger, more muscular, than he had remembered. The muscles under his T-shirt rippled when he extended his arm to shake Jared's hand, and his grip was rock hard. Even that cocky spark was back in his eyes.

"You look good," said Jared.

"And you like you've been eating too much rice and raw fish. Didn't they feed you any real food in Japan? Sheesh, I'm going to have to put you on a training program to whip you back into shape before any girls get a look at your pale, wimpy body."

Rob sat next to Jared. "So how was it? Are you glad you went?"

"It was great, really great, but not at all what I expected. It's the kind of experience that's hard to describe, really."

"What about Japan?"

"What's with all the questions? Didn't you read my letters? If you had really wanted more detail about my life in Japan," Jared punched him in the shoulder, "you could have written a letter or two."

Rob blushed. "Yeah, well, I know I should have written you more often . . ."

"More often? You can't use 'more often' to describe something that never happened."

"OK, I should have written you, but I was kind of messed up for a while after you left. No, *really* messed up. By the time I got my head on straight, I hadn't written you for so long that I was too embarrassed to write. I meant to, though, really."

"So how are things?"

"Coming from a freshly returned missionary, I assume 'things' means me and the Church. Well," Rob sighed, "like I said, things were pretty rocky for a while. I even moved out for a few months just to see what was what. But the problem was, I had no clue what I was looking for. All I knew was that I was miserable, but I couldn't figure out what was making me miserable, so I ended up being pretty much a pain to everybody around me.

"But you know, my dad's cool, and he hung in there with me—even visited my place a couple times—and didn't preach or yell at me. He kept telling me that he knew I had made some mistakes, but that wasn't the end of the world. Finally I got hungry enough and tired enough of feeling lousy, and I came home. It hasn't been easy, but 'things' got better."

Jared felt like a light had turned on. "You know, there were some times on my mission that were pretty hard, and when I got depressed from people ignoring me, from freezing to death in the winter, sweating to death in the summer, from broken appointments, from being thousands of miles away from home, I thought about you and all that happened, and I realized that I wasn't the only guy having a hard time. And that's the great thing about repentance. I had this one companion—"

"Whoa, dude, don't start with the mission tales already."

"But I just wanted to tell you about—"

Rob poked Jared in the ribs. "Back off, buddy. You're not on a mission anymore, so there's no reason to start preaching to me. Look, I'll be at your homecoming tomorrow, and I'll listen to all the mission tales you want to tell. Deal?"

"Deal." Jared slapped Rob's outstretched hand.

"So how's your old man?"

"Haven't seen him yet. He's out on a job. But I've still got a place to live, which is a little surprising. Mom says he hasn't changed, and that's no surprise."

"How do you handle *that?* I mean, I can't imagine my dad treating me like that."

Jared shrugged. "He's my dad, and even though I don't like what he does, I've learned that I can still love him . . . that I do love him."

Rob just looked at him and shook his head. For a moment, neither spoke; then Rob asked, "You ever think about her?"

"Leisel?"

Rob nodded.

Jared sighed. "All the time."

"I'm really sorry, Jared." Rob's eyes turned misty. "Sorry for the accident, for acting like a jerk afterwards. I've carried that weight around for a long time and I've been through hell the last couple years, but I've finally gotten rid of it. You don't have to forgive me and I'll understand, but I just want you to know that I really am sorry."

"I wish it had never happened," Jared said. "I wish that Leisel had been there at the airport to greet me, but I forgave you a long time ago. I hope you've finally forgiven yourself."

Rob looked down without answering. He wiped his eyes with the back of his hand and said, "Thanks. Thanks a lot."

Jared and his mother ate dinner alone that night because his father was still out of town. Neither knew how long it would be until he returned.

"Has Dad been traveling a lot lately?" asked Jared.

"Just before you came back, he started working more nights and weekends. You know I hate what he does, but I don't know what I can do about it. He just refuses to listen to reason."

"He can be pretty stubborn."

"I don't know what to do." She pushed her plate back and sighed. "You must be ashamed of him, especially now that you've served a mission for your church and all. I just ask that you tolerate him, try to get along. I want you to stay home, to live with us, but I'm afraid your father will drive you away. And I have no hope that he'll ever change."

Jared could see how badly his mother wanted things to work out. "You know, my last companion was a real wimp, a crybaby. That first night," he smiled at the memory, "I thought he'd drive me crazy, and I was sure there was no way we'd last a week. I knew he wasn't going to change. He'd been a momma's boy all his life, and there was nothing I could do to change him. Then I decided to change myself. My mission taught me that I could love people who acted in ways I didn't like."

"But your father . . ."

"I know Dad's a hard case, but I think I can handle it. At least I'm sure I want to give it a try."

Jared's homecoming went pretty much as he expected. He loved being in a familiar ward full of familiar faces. The Lees, as always, lined the fourth row. Brother Speares and other members of the elders quorum who had supported Jared were also there. But this meeting was unlike most church meetings Jared had attended because dead center in the second row sat Rob Whitman.